# TRAVELLE

# MALDIVES

By
**DEBBIE STOWE**

**Written by Debbie Stowe**
Original photography by Vasile Szakacs

**Published by Thomas Cook Publishing**
A division of Thomas Cook Tour Operations Limited.
Company registration no. 1450464 England
The Thomas Cook Business Park, 9 Coningsby Road,
Peterborough PE3 8SB, United Kingdom
E-mail: sales@thomascook.com, Tel: + 44 (0) 1733 416477
www.thomascookpublishing.com

**Produced by Cambridge Publishing Management Limited**
Burr Elm Court, Main Street, Caldecote CB23 7NU

ISBN: 978-1-84157-821-7

Text © 2008 Thomas Cook Publishing
Maps © 2008 Thomas Cook Publishing/PCGraphics (UK) Limited

Series Editor: Maisie Fitzpatrick
Production/DTP: Steven Collins

Printed and bound in Italy by Printer Trento

Cover photography: Front L–R: © Picpics/Alamy; © Amos Nachoum/CORBIS;
© Borchi Massimo/4Corners Images. Back L–R: © Michael Hayward; © Ron
Dahlquist/Photolibrary.com

The paper used for this book has been independently certified as having
been sourced from well-managed forests and recycled wood or fibre
according to the rules of the Forest Stewardship Council.
This book has been printed and bound in Italy by Printer Trento S.r.l.,
an FSC certified company for printing books on FSC mixed paper in
compliance with the chain of custody and on products labelling standards.

**FSC**

**Mixed Sources**
Product group from well-managed
forests and recycled wood or fibre

Cert no. CQ-COC-000012
www.fsc.org
© 1996 Forest Stewardship Council

# Contents

| Background | 4–19 |
| --- | --- |
| Introduction | 4 |
| The land | 6 |
| History | 8 |
| Politics | 12 |
| Culture | 14 |
| Festivals and events | 18 |

| Highlights | 20–25 |
| --- | --- |
| Highlights | 20 |
| Suggested itineraries | 23 |

| Destination guide | 26–105 |
| --- | --- |
| Male | 26 |
| North Male Atoll | 44 |
| South Male Atoll | 58 |
| Ari Atoll | 72 |
| Northern Atolls | 86 |
| Southern Atolls | 96 |

| Getting away from it all | 106–9 |
| --- | --- |

| Practical guide | 110–43 |
| --- | --- |
| When to go | 110 |
| Getting around | 112 |
| Accommodation | 116 |
| Food and drink | 118 |
| Entertainment | 122 |
| Shopping | 126 |
| Sport and leisure | 128 |
| Children | 132 |
| Essentials | 134 |
| Emergencies | 142 |

| Directory | 144–57 |
| --- | --- |

| Index | 158–9 |
| --- | --- |

| Maps | |
| --- | --- |
| The land | 7 |
| Highlights | 20 |
| Male | 27 |
| Walk: Male centre | 29 |
| North Male Atoll | 45 |
| Walk: Villingili | 55 |
| South Male Atoll | 59 |
| One of the *Atoll Explorer*'s routes | 69 |
| Ari Atoll | 73 |
| Tour: Scenic seaplane | 83 |
| Northern Atolls | 87 |
| Southern Atolls | 97 |
| Tour: Gan and Seenu Atoll | 103 |

| Features | |
| --- | --- |
| Islam in the Maldives | 10 |
| Cowries | 30 |
| Atoll formation | 42 |
| Black magic | 56 |
| Wildlife | 66 |
| Environmentalism | 70 |
| Coral reefs | 84 |
| Diving | 94 |
| Fish | 104 |

| Tours and walks | |
| --- | --- |
| Walk: Male centre | 28 |
| Walk: Villingili | 54 |
| Tour: Island-hopping | 64 |
| Tour: Island cruises | 68 |
| Tour: Scenic seaplane | 82 |
| Tour: Gan and Seenu Atoll | 102 |

# Introduction

*Getting away from it all doesn't come much more absolute than in the Maldives. Desert islands more commonly the stuff of legend, literature or the imagination are so plentiful here that they reach four figures, with the only additions being the minimum of amenities required to ensure the visitor's every holiday need will be met. As a beach destination, the country has all the clichés – pristine sands, warm crystal waters, photogenic palm trees, impeccable service, hot weather and great food.*

What distinguishes it from some comparable resorts in the region is the eye that the developers have kept on the relentless rise of tourism and its accoutrements. The folksy law that no resort building should stand higher than the tallest palm tree, along with the geographical limitations of island

Palm trees on Royal Island

size, have prohibited the unchecked consumerism that purists bemoan in Goa and its ilk. Maldivian resorts are quiet (the rowdiest things get would be a group of cabin crew enjoying their stopover), safe (everyone in your resort will be either a staff member or a guest) and professional, ensuring plenty of repeat visitors and honeymooners, plus couples on their holiday of a lifetime.

Unlike the sometimes sloppy or endearingly amateur service and facilities the traveller might encounter in India or Sri Lanka, the two nearest countries, hospitality in the Maldives is impeccable. Tourism here has been developed in a controlled way, and a decision was made to cater for the upmarket tourist. A 'cheap' resort in the Maldives would be a perfectly decent 3-star hotel elsewhere. Everything has been thought through and organised with the greatest efficiency. In the hotel, the cleaning process is almost constant, so rooms, facilities and beach are all immaculate. It is hard to imagine

Translucent waters and a near-deserted beach on Sun Island

friendlier service, with guests and staff exchanging pleasant greetings to such an extent that on your return home it feels strange to walk past someone else without saying hello. And the food – most guests eat exclusively on their resort islands – will satisfy everyone from the adventurous gastronome who wants to go native to the resolute homebody sticking to his or her national cuisine.

This level of control has just one drawback. In the government's anxiety not to let the tourists' Western ways infect the local population, the infrastructure and set-up make it very difficult to see how native Maldivians – aside from resort employees – really live. With the exception of Male and one of its neighbouring islands, and the rather stage-managed island-hopping tours offered by hotels, it is extremely difficult if not unfeasible for the average holidaymaker to see an authentic inhabited island. It is possible to come to the Maldives, spend your two weeks here and leave without learning anything about the national character or culture, eating the food, or even handling the local currency. Sunseekers may be quite happy with this, but to the curious traveller it is the one obvious omission in an otherwise complete package. If you do manage to make the breakthrough and get to know the Maldivians, you will find a people that seems to belong not quite in the Indian subcontinent, not quite among the Islamic nations, not quite among the typical tourist destinations, but to somewhere unique, protected from the outside world by miles and miles of aquatic seclusion.

# The land

*With over 99 per cent of its territory consisting of seawater, very little of the Maldives can be described as land. Of the 1,192 islands (many Maldivians claim the total is far higher), around 200 are inhabited by local people, fewer than 100 (but rising) have been turned into resorts and the rest remain the classic image of the desert island: small, sandy and adorned with little more than a clutch of palm trees.*

The islands are spread over an area of 822km × 130km (510 miles × 80 miles) at its widest point, and are divided into 22 atolls – oceanic reef formations created when coral reef develops around a volcanic island, which subsequently sinks into the sea – plus a few other islands that can be considered smaller atoll formations. All of the islands are tiny: the largest is 8sq km (3sq miles).

Islanders are fighting an unremitting battle using sandbags and supports to keep the sea at bay; it continuously erodes their beaches and deposits the sand elsewhere. The problem is particularly acute in the crowded capital Male.

With the exception of Male and its concrete, the rest of the terrain is almost entirely sand. The islands are flat and low-lying, with no rivers or mountains and few lakes. Some islands are impressively verdant – due both to the tropical conditions and to resort managers importing soil and plants to beautify their patch of sand – and provide much-needed shade. The trees that grow on the islands tend to have a practical function and are used for timber, windbreaks, firewood, fruit and other day-to-day products.

### BREAKING RECORDS

Little about the Maldives could ever be described as ordinary, and the country either holds or is high in the ranking for several geographical records. Not only does its capital challenge Mumbai as the world's most densely populated city, but the country is the flattest in the world, with its highest point just 2.4m (almost 8ft) above sea level. In 2006 it broke the existing record for the most people scuba-diving simultaneously – slightly under 1,000.

A view of a Maldivian island from a seaplane

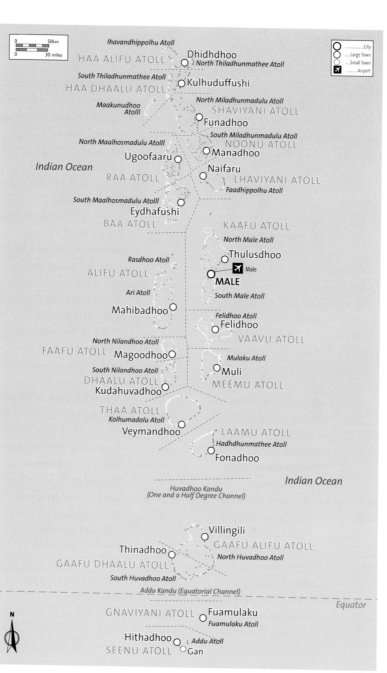

# History

**c. 500 BC**  Aryan immigrants establish settlements in the Maldives.

**c. 300 BC**  Buddhism spreads to the Maldives and becomes the dominant religion.

**AD 362**  Embassy sent from the Maldives to Roman Emperor Julian.

**AD 851**  Early reference to the islands in Arab travel chronicles.

**1153**  The Maldives adopts Islam (*see panel, p141*) and the Buddhist king becomes Sultan Mohamed Ibn Abdulla. The Maldives will be presided over by Islamic dynasties for the next eight centuries.

**1498**  Vasco da Gama reaches Calicut, India, heralding the start of an era of unprecedented tyranny for the Maldives.

**1503**  Portuguese leader Vicente Sodre prohibits trade between the Maldives and Calicut.

**1558**  Sultan Hassan IX flees to India after a disagreement with the council of elders and converts to Christianity. He returns to the country as an invader, helped by the Portuguese, and takes Male. The occupation lasts 15 years, during which the ruler tries to convert the local people to Christianity.

**1573**  After eight years of trying, Maldivian guerrillas liberate Male with help from the Malabars of southern India. The leader of the resistance, Mohamed Thakurufaanu, becomes sultan. During his 12-year reign he reforms the government and legal system, establishes an efficient army, introduces coins instead of cowrie shells and begins trade with foreign countries.

**1609**  Malabars attack Male and kill the sultan but fail to take the town.

**1624 & 1648**  Portuguese unsuccessfully attempt to retake control of the country.

| | |
|---|---|
| **1650** | In an unprecedented display of aggression and following two attempted invasions by the Rajah of Cannanore, the Maldivian sultan, Ibrahim Iskandhar invades the Indian city and takes some hostages. The situation is resolved with payment of a ransom. In a reign of nearly four decades, the sultan builds the Friday Mosque and the first public school. |
| **1690** | The Malabars again attempt to invade the Maldives. |
| **1711 & 1712** | Six years after he was deposed, Sultan Ibrahim Muzhiruddin attacks his own country with Indian support. |
| **1752** | Malabars make several attacks on Male until Dhon Hassan Manikufaan calls in French forces as a deterrent. |
| **1759** | Dhon Hassan Manikufaan succeeds the previous ruler after his death in 1757. The Huraage dynasty he founded goes on to rule, with just one brief interruption, for nearly two centuries. |
| **1887** | Maldives becomes a protected state of Britain but is permitted to run its own affairs without interference. |
| **1932** | First written constitution proclaimed. |
| **1953** | Country declared a republic with Mohamed Ameen Didi as president. |
| **1954** | Death of the country's first president, following some unrest, leads to the sultanate being restored. |
| **1965** | Maldives gains independence from Britain and joins the United Nations. |
| **1968** | Sultanate abolished again and a president elected. |
| **1972** | First tourist resort opens. |
| **1976** | British complete withdrawal of forces. |
| **1978** | Maumoon Abdul Gayoom elected president. |
| **2020** | Vision 2020 is the name for an ambitious set of projects hoped to improve the country's social, economic and world standing. |

# Islam in the Maldives

As you relax on the beach, a cocktail in hand, it is hard to conceive of the Maldives as a theocratic state. But not only is Islam the official religion, it is also obligatory for all citizens to adhere to it. Sharia forms the basis of the local law, which often jars with the country's efforts to develop as a forward-looking nation (such as when two top Dhivehi actors were publicly whipped in 2002 after being caught in an adulterous relationship).

Every island has a mosque, some have more than one and Male is said to have a staggering 30-plus, all within an area of less than 2.5sq km (1sq mile). Although there are some exceptions, the vast majority of Maldivians are Sunni Muslims. The custodian of religion in the country is the president.

Maldivians are called to prayer five times every day, and shops and offices close for around a quarter of an hour following the call. Even television programmes, including foreign channels, stop broadcasting. Friday is the holy day, and on village islands things begin to wind down at around 11am, allowing everyone to get to the mosque in time for the service at around 12.30pm. But Islam most makes its presence felt throughout the month of Ramadan, when working hours are reduced and cafés and restaurants close during daylight hours.

Staying on a resort island, you may not even notice the country's religious system; the government does not want to risk doing anything to deter tourists, and foreigners are exempt from most of the religious requirements. Alcohol, for example, can be consumed copiously by tourists but is forbidden for the local people. Attempt to import any drink and it will be confiscated; the consequences for a Maldivian caught drinking would be far worse. Other items deemed un-Islamic, and therefore prohibited, include pigs (although pork is served in resorts), dogs, pornography, and any non-Islamic religious paraphernalia.

Minaret of a mosque in Male

Prayer mats neatly stacked outside a mosque

But despite the seemingly draconian aspects of Islam in the country, there are several incongruities that prevent the Maldives being categorised with other theocracies. The main one is the religion's co-existence with a variety of other beliefs in the spirit world and black magic (*see pp56–7*). Even the story of how Islam first came to be adopted in the country, with its demons and virgins (*see panel, p141*), seems to owe more to allegory than accuracy. With the Maldives geographically so isolated, faith on the islands has developed without significant cultural influence from other nations, and many islanders seem laid-back about their religion.

Anthropologist Clarence Maloney, who studied the country in the 1970s, writes about a Muslim cleric who told him that for the majority of Maldivians, Islam was 'largely a matter of observing ablutions, fasting, and reciting incomprehensible Arabic prayer formulas' (*People of the Maldive Islands*, 1980). They were taught the Koran from childhood and gave little thought to other options. For many today, it is clear that religious pluralism has not been a success elsewhere, and they are quite happy with their peaceful, if restrictive, status quo, and attribute the lack of crime in their country to the didactic and sobering influence of Islam.

# Politics

*As an independent democracy, the Maldives is relatively young. After centuries as a sultanate, it was under the influence of the British from the end of the 19th century until the mid-1960s, shortly before the system of sultans was abandoned (twice) in favour of an elected president. How different this is from the old way is debatable; voters do not have the option of two competing politicians but just vote 'yes' or 'no' to the sole candidate proposed, and in nearly 40 years the country has had only two presidents.*

Since 1153 the country has lived under Islamic Sharia law. Practical constraints have prevented too much central intervention in island affairs, so individual areas have had significant responsibility for self-rule, a system that seems to have worked well.

Today, the country is divided into 20 administrative units, which, although demarcated geographically and known as atolls, do not exactly correspond with the physical atolls themselves. Each one is run by an island chief and elects two members of parliament, who sit in Male. Assisted by a small team of officials, the chief commands considerable respect from the islanders, and he (or she – one woman has been appointed to the role) and his colleagues are able to sort out most problems independently, without recourse to the National Security Service police force. The *Majlis* (parliament) consists of the 40 members from the islands plus a further eight nominated by the president, giving the latter a significant degree of influence over the institution and its proceedings.

Both parliamentary and presidential elections are held every five years, but not at the same time. While, theoretically, any Maldivian man (but not woman) can now put himself forward for consideration as a

The Maldivian flag flies proudly high above the people

The old presidential palace in Male

presidential candidate to be voted on by MPs, the electoral landscape has been dominated by two men ever since its inception; the first president Ibrahim Nasir, who held power from 1968–78,

### PRESIDENT GAYOOM

The Maldivian president, Maumoon Abdul Gayoom, is certainly a divisive figure. While many Maldivians credit him with their country's recent economic progress and stability, others view him as a nepotistic dictator, siphoning off power and the profits of the burgeoning tourism industry into the pockets of his family and coterie of cronies. Despite the criticism, which is largely silenced within the Maldives itself, Gayoom was re-elected in 2003 – for his sixth five-year term – with over 90 per cent of the vote, making him Asia's longest-serving leader. Never one to underestimate his own capabilities, he also served as defence and finance minister until stepping down owing to international pressure and public ridicule.

and the present president, Maumoon Abdul Gayoom (*see panel*).

While some Maldivians are pleased with the stability the country has enjoyed under Gayoom, he has also been criticised for running an autocratic, repressive regime and in some parts is considered a dictator. In 2005, parliament voted to introduce a multi-party democracy, although this is taking a long time to realise, with the first multi-party elections not expected until 2008.

The Maldivian Democratic Party is the main voice calling for change. It is supported by, but not affiliated to, the *Dhiveli Observer*, a news and information website set up in the UK and banned in the Maldives (*www.dhiveli-observer.com*). So far the Gayoom regime has kept a tight reign over the media.

# Culture

*The demands of island living have long taken priority over the arts in the Maldives, and this, coupled with the inherent difficulties of communication and association, have prevented a flourishing arts scene from developing. Those disciplines that do have a tradition have it through necessity. Mat-weaving and lacquerware are the main two examples of a craft developing for utilitarian reasons, as well as architecture. Literature and cinema have a limited history, while legend and music have long played a role in alleviating island boredom.*

## Architecture

Male and the Maldives are now seeing the same changes as all developing countries, with new buildings replacing traditional structures to meet the demands of modern life, particularly in the capital. However, odd pockets of older architecture do remain. Coral and coconut, two Maldivian staples, formed the basis of a house; coral stone was used to build a platform and coconut wood was used for the superstructure. Owing to the Maldivians' skills in assembling boats, they were able to build wooden houses and form tight joints without using nails. The design

The entrance to a mosque in Villingili

of the typical house – built around a hall that led to a *malem* (reception room), where the man of the house would meet male guests, with the rest of the property being off limits to outsiders – sheds some light on local concepts of privacy and gender roles.

The other main theme in Maldivian structural design is mosque architecture. Religious buildings have changed little since the 17th century. Typically a mosque is made of stone (wood is less common), and raised on a rectangular platform with an entrance to the east and a recess to the west. A well is found outside near the door, and the buildings are surrounded by a graveyard of coral tombstones, a rounded top indicating the grave of a woman and a pointed top for a man. *Mihrabs* (the niche in the wall indicating the direction of prayer) and minarets are rare.

Local clay jars on display at Aaramu Spa

## Cinema

The Maldivian film industry, better known as Dhivehi after the national language, is just 30 years old, and most films are broadcast solely in the state-run Olympus Cinema in Male. About ten films are made each year. Features tend to follow the Bollywood model, and some are direct remakes of Indian productions.

Despite the limitations imposed by government censorship and an Islamic regime, some film-makers are now starting to use their art to tackle various taboo subjects, such as impotency, loveless marriage and violence against women. The state is now supporting local film-makers – though not without controversy – and the country stages occasional film industry awards.

## Crafts

Like many Maldivian crafts, mats have strong associations with particular islands. The women of Gadhdhoo, in Gaafu Dhaalu Atoll, are the manufacturers of the country's most famous mats, called *thundu kunaa*. *Haa* (reeds) are collected from Fioari, an island in the vicinity, left to dry in the heat of the sun and then dyed naturally in shades from fawn to black. The reeds are then woven into red mats with abstract designs.

Lacquerware, meanwhile, has its roots predominantly in Thulhaadhoo

A Villingili woman in traditional dress with her child

folklore dates back to ancient times, and has been passed down orally from one generation to the next. The stories were designed to entertain but also to instruct; spirits often punished bad behaviour and rewarded more desirable qualities, thus deterring villagers from contravening island norms. Myths explain everything from the origin of the capital city and the nation's conversion to Islam to its predestined demise (it is predicted to disappear under the ocean – something that environmentalists fear may be more than just a myth). Quite understandably, given the crucial role that the natural world – particularly the ocean – plays in island life, much of the mythology relates to sailors, the sea, marine life and the other creatures and plants on which Maldivian life is contingent.

in Baa Atoll. Pieces of wood from the local *funa* (Alexandrian laurel) are shaped and hollowed out to form boxes, vases and ornaments in a process called *liye laajehun*. The objects are then lacquered in strands of coloured resin and carved with floral patterns.

## Legend and folklore

The things that have limited the development of other branches of the arts, such as lack of communication with the outside world, have allowed legend and folklore to thrive. Maldivian

## Literature

Before the 20th century, Maldivian literature consisted largely of handwritten texts, usually featuring a traditional form of poetry, which rarely enjoyed much distribution. The archaic form of Dhivehi used, which was closer to Sinhalese, is incomprehensible today to the majority of Maldivians. The medium developed along with the arrival of the printing press in the early 20th century, and this period also saw the first Dhivehi novel, the creation of *lhen*, a formal style of poetry, and the use of imagery in prose.

The advent of the internet effected another revolution in Maldivian literature, coming as it did with a recent law enshrining freedom of speech. But local access to international culture through the internet has also worked against national literature, as young writers are beginning to abandon their national language to write in English and, to a lesser extent, Arabic. Some believe that these authors' imperfect use of their chosen language has resulted in a decline in quality. On the other hand, the adoption of English by some writers does give their books – and therefore Maldivian literature – a potentially wider audience than the estimated national population of 370,000.

## Music and dance

Through seafaring exchanges with the peoples of surrounding nations of India, Africa, Arabia, Malaysia and Indonesia, local music has been shaped by a salad of racial influences. Its best-known manifestation is *Bodu Beru* (or *Baburu Lava*, 'Negroid song'), which is said to have been introduced to the islands by African sailors a thousand years ago and shares elements with East African folk music. A performance consists of a group of around fifteen men, including three drummers, a lead singer, bell ringer and someone scraping a bamboo instrument, singing songs of heroism, love or humour, which start slowly and come to a frenetic denouement, sometimes culminating in a trance. The lyrics were traditionally a jumble of national, regional and African words, but now the Maldivian language of Dhivehi may be used instead.

The country has a variety of dances to go with *Bodu Beru*, with some variation between atolls. *Thaara* (tambourine) was brought to the Maldives by Gulf Arabs in the 17th century, and *Gaa Odi Lava* is performed following hard manual labour to convey satisfaction. Young people and women also have their own dances, and they may be performed to ward off illness, celebrate festivals, tell stories, or merely for fun.

Traditional drums on display in a shop in Villingili

# Festivals and events

*Owing to the Maldives' intertwining of church and autocratic state, the country does not celebrate much unless Islam or patriotism is at the heart of it. But when they do celebrate, the Maldivians do so with panache. Much of the time the country seems to have little in common with India and Sri Lanka, its nearest neighbours, but when it comes to celebrating, all the colour of the sub-continent is in evidence in vibrant parades, music and costumes.*

The following festivals are based on the lunar Islamic calendar, so the timing of the events varies from year to year.

**Ramadan**, the fourth pillar of Islam, is the most important event in the religious calendar, and is observed strictly in the Maldives. The festival, known in the archipelago as *Roadhamas*, consists of a month of fasting between sunrise and sunset, plus the renouncing of all worldly pleasures. Restaurants do not open during this period. (Resort life, however, remains unaffected and resort island restaurants

The Islamic Center in Male also houses a mosque

operate as normal.) Ramadan is the ninth month of the Islamic year.

The end of the month is marked by **Eid**, which is celebrated understandably joyfully. The sultan's procession of yesteryear, replete with drums, music and military displays, has its modern day equivalent in concerts, brass bands and cadet and National Security Service demonstrations. Other celebrations vary from island to island and Eid to Eid (one marks the end of Ramadan, the other the end of the Hajj pilgrimage to Mecca).

**National Day** commemorates the victory of Mohamed Thakurufaanu over the Portuguese occupiers in 1573, ending what was probably the worst 15 years in Maldivian history. Street parades in Male and around the islands are held to celebrate the occasion.

**Mohamed's birthday** sees Muslims (i.e. everyone) go to the mosque early in the morning. The rest of the festival, which lasts three days, is spent at home or at the house of family or friends, enjoying the public holiday with a large

A traditional band sings on the beach at Banyan Tree

feast. It starts on the 12th day of the third month of the Muslim calendar.

## July

Commemorating the day when the Maldives won full autonomy from Britain on 26 July 1965, **Independence Day** celebrations typically involve a lot of pomp and pageantry. President Gayoom usually has a big hand in proceedings, and gives an address to his people, with foreign dignitaries invited along for the occasion. Parades, marching bands, brightly coloured floats and costumes are also part of the fun.

## November

In 1988, Tamil mercenaries tried to overthrow the government. The attempted coup was thwarted with help from India, but not before many local people were killed in the crossfire. They are commemorated on **Victory Day**, 3 November.

**Republic Day** celebrates the day the country became a republic for the second time on 11 November 1968. Parades, marches and meetings are held to mark the occasion, while at home women, men and children pitch in together to prepare the decorations, food and entertainment, as is common for most events of this kind. Some concessions to modernity have been made; today's festivities see pop music played alongside traditional folk music and dances.

# Highlights

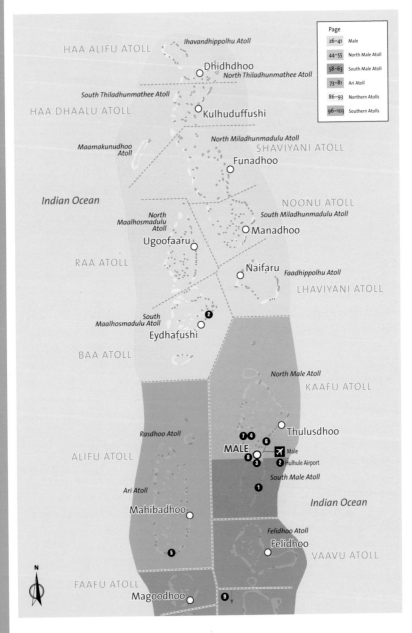

Page

| 26–41 | Male |
| 44–55 | North Male Atoll |
| 58–63 | South Male Atoll |
| 73–81 | Ari Atoll |
| 86–93 | Northern Atolls |
| 96–103 | Southern Atolls |

**❶ Seafood at Cocoa Island**
The one foodstuff that the Maldives is teeming with, delectable fresh fish, tastes its best when there's sand beneath your feet and you're looking out to sea.

**❷ Flight by sea plane from Male to Soneva Fushi in North Baa Atoll** The extraordinary geography of this island nation is best appreciated from the skies.

**❸ Snorkelling and diving at Vadhoo Caves** Warm, clear, safe waters and a cornucopia of sea creatures going about their business just below the surface explain why divers love the Maldives as much as honeymooners do.

**❹ Watching turtle and stingray feeding at Banyan Tree**
The Banyan Tree's ecological programmes bring the weird and wonderful aquatic world right to the beach.

**❺ Water villas at Sun Island**
Leave your room via a ladder straight down to the sea for an authentic holiday on the water.

A seaplane lands at Hulhule Airport

**6 Listening to live music on the beach at night at Paradise Island** With cabin crew making the most of their stopover and letting their hair down, beach parties at Paradise are about as lively as the Maldives ever gets.

**7 Massage in the resort spa at Angsana** The back-to-nature resort is an ideal setting to indulge yourself with massages inspired by techniques from three continents.

**8 Islamic architecture in Male** In a crowded capital that is increasingly choked with modernity, mosques and the occasional minaret provide glimpses of aesthetic peace.

**9 Village life in Gan** Boasting the sole holiday resort in the country where you share your patch of land with Maldivians other than hotel employees, Gan is a favourite destination with backpackers and other independent travellers seeking to get more than the usual pristine sands and cocktails from their trip.

**10 Friendliness of the local people** Never again will you exchange so many amiable greetings with so many strangers during a holiday, whether resort employees or simply sociable locals.

Feeding stingrays at Banyan Tree Resort

# Suggested itineraries

Although some Asian tourists do come to the Maldives for a long weekend, the distance and jetlag faced by European visitors make a week the minimum time needed to enjoy your holiday. At first glance, the islands may seem to differ little, and boredom seems inevitable on a longer stay. But resorts make a great effort to distinguish their facilities and keep their guests entertained, and when it's time to return home, most holidaymakers will find themselves wishing for a few extra days.

## One week

On a week-long trip you won't want the hassle of switching resorts. A week's package to a resort in North or South Male Atoll will mean you're near enough to the capital for a day or half-day trip, which can be spent sight-seeing, shopping or a bit of both. Another two days can be given over to the excursions offered by your hotel. Island-hopping will give you a taste of village life, and to enjoy the ocean environment there's fishing, whale- and dolphin-spotting or

A modern tourist boat moored in Male

Suggested itineraries

diving. For a proper rest, the remaining days can be spent around the resort, swimming, snorkelling and sunbathing.

**Two weeks**

With two weeks you have a few more choices. Financially, it still makes sense to book a package. You could stay for nearly all of the two weeks on an island, and extend your time in Male (perhaps staying overnight in a hotel in the capital to experience a bustling city evening). If you're keen to visit another island, this now becomes easier to arrange, and you can try more of the hotel excursions as well.

Another option is to stick with one week at a resort, and with the rest of your time cruise around the island, either by chartering a vessel yourself (known as a safari boat) or booking a berth on a scheduled cruise such as the *Atoll Explorer* (*see panel, p93*). Not only will you be able to see much more of

the Maldives than you could while staying in one resort, but you can also enjoy the sociability or privacy, as you prefer, of boat life.

Such a jaunt is likely to start and end in Male, and you can have a day or two exploring the capital too, now with time to see the museum and visit a nearby island – Villingili is the closest. Divers in particular may prefer to spend some of their holiday time staying on a boat, as some cruises cater specifically for them and tour some of the country's best and more remote dive sites.

**Longer**

Few visitors stay longer than two weeks, but a trip of this duration really allows you to see the country and get well away from the tourist areas. You'll have plenty of time to relax at a resort if you take a package deal, and could even split your time between two hotels – a livelier one near Male and a more peaceful, remote one. You could go on a cruise or even two, perhaps a scheduled one with other tourists and then a few days exploring on a chartered vessel alone.

Male merits two or three days at least, which can be spent leisurely exploring and experiencing much more of the local life. A longer trip also gives you the time to arrange a visit to a remoter island, which requires research and battling bureaucracy that might be burdensome on a shorter visit.

### KOIMALA KALOA, THE LEGEND OF HABITATION

The famed passivity of the Maldivian people is illustrated in the legend of habitation. The story is about Prince Koimala and his wife, the daughter of the King of Serendib (the old Arabic name for Sri Lanka). One day they set sail, and after a long time reached the Maldives, where they disembarked on the island of Rasgetheemu in Raa Atoll. When the residents of the nearby isles learned of his royal blood they proclaimed him king. Later, Koimala saw a white bird flying overhead on successive days. He followed it by boat, and it eventually led him to Male, which he then declared his new home.

The crew at work on a tourist-boat trip

# Male

*Ask an island-based Maldivian what the country's capital city is like, and your answer is likely to come in the form of a small frown and the words 'hot' or 'crowded'. In a largely homogeneous country, a visit to Male comes as a culture shock. Go there on a day trip from your resort island, where hustle and bustle are unheard of and the only engine you're likely to hear will be from a speedboat or motorised* dhoni, *and the capital will seem a chaotic metropolis, teeming with industry, noise and traffic.*

Of course, Male's commotion pales in comparison with its closest equivalents, Delhi and Sri Lanka. The streets are seldom clogged with vehicles, although that's not to say it doesn't sometimes feel crowded. With a third of the country's population, about 75,000 people, crammed into an area of 2.5sq km (1sq mile), it is said to be the world's most densely populated city and it certainly feels like it. A glance at the cityscape belies the country's theocratic regime; only the golden dome of the **Islamic Centre** suggests the intrusion of religion into a thoroughly modern city.

## Orientation

Visitors are likely to arrive next to the Presidential Jetty at the north of the island, or at the northeast corner if coming from the airport. Most of the highlights are clustered in this section, which means that as little as an hour or two's exploration can take in quite a bit. The main thoroughfares run north-south and east-west, but there is a warren of intersecting smaller streets that are worth a wander, particularly as they have a more authentic, ad hoc Maldivian feel. The best and almost only possible way to see the city is by foot. The adventurous might be tempted to hire a bicycle or motorbike, although the traffic will deter many, and older tourists or anyone whose mobility is too limited for jumping out of the way of passing motorbikes may prefer an air-conditioned taxi.

Male viewed from the air

## History

Always the country's political and cultural heart, Male was developed significantly under the Portuguese during their 15 years of occupation in the 16th century, in large part because of the daunting reputation of their Armada elsewhere, which foreign sailors hoped to avoid by charting their course through the Maldives. Even before then, the island was used as a mid-ocean stopping-off point for boats on their way between South East Asia, East Africa and Arabia. The seamen who pitched up would also take the opportunity to conduct some trade, picking up fish and other Maldivian produce, and many formed links of a more permanent kind by marrying local women.

The island's name comes from the Sanskrit word *mahaalay*, which means 'big house', although a legend about the town's origins posits a different theory. In this story, fishermen from the nearby island of Giravaru used a local sandbank to clean their catch, with the effect that it was often surrounded by blood. When a prince called Koimala (*see panel, p24*) arrived from the subcontinent, he resided on the sandbank and in time the people agreed for him to rule over them. While the story's accuracy is impossible to establish, it points to the other interpretation of the Sanskrit name as 'big blood'.

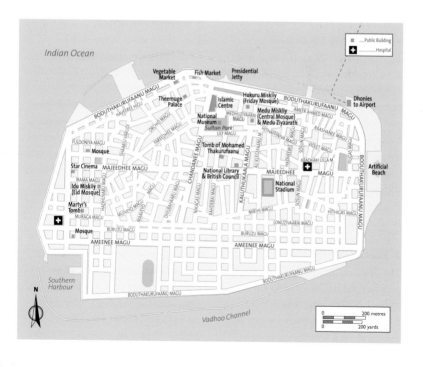

# Walk: Male centre

*Male in itself is a tiny capital, and its main highlights are concentrated in a small area to the north of the island. Given the almost constant heat, it's advisable to leave enough time for this stroll not to have to rush.*

*Allow two hours, but leave longer if you want to stop off at any of the sights or break for shopping or refreshments. The total distance covered is less than a kilometre (²/₃ mile), or slightly over if you walk around the park.*

*Starting from near the Presidential Jetty, your likely point of arrival if you're coming from a resort island, you will see a public garden, the Jumhooree Maidhaan, opposite you on the other side of the road.*

## 1 Jumhooree Maidhaan

The tree-lined borders of this park are often crowded with local people trying to escape the sun. At other times, it serves as a location for public demonstrations and protests. The large Maldivian flag flying at the east end of the park serves as a useful orientation point.
*Cross Jumhooree Maidhaan, veering slightly to your right. The large building in front of you is the unmistakeable Islamic Centre.*

## 2 Islamic Centre

The Maldives' largest and most famous architectural landmark is the three-storey Islamic Centre, which has a 5,000-worshipper capacity prayer hall, conference hall and library (*see pp32–3*).

*Pass the Islamic Centre and continue in the same direction you've been walking since the start, and you will come to the modern monument called the Jumhooree Binaa.*

## 3 Jumhooree Binaa

This statue, also known as the Republican Monument, has been in place since 1999, when it was unveiled to commemorate the 30th anniversary of the Second Republic, albeit a year late. A contemporary and challenging design visually, it was put together with help from local students.
*Immediately opposite the roundabout on which the Jumhooree Binaa sits is the entrance to Sultan Park.*

## 4 Sultan Park

The park is a pleasant mix of paved walkways and green areas (*see pp40–41*).
*Come out of the park the same way you entered it and turn right. After about 100m (330ft) you will see Hukuru Miskiiy (Friday Mosque) on your left.*

## 5 Hukuru Miskiiy (Friday Mosque)

The Friday Mosque, one of the most atmospheric and ornate in the country, was built in 1656 and features *munnaaru*, a minaret that dates back to the same period, which was for centuries used to make the call to prayer, before the honour passed to the Islamic Centre (*see pp32–3*).

*Immediately opposite Hukuru Miskiiy, to the south, is Mulee-Aage.*

## 6 Mulee-Aage (former Presidential Palace)

This bright and cheerful blue and white building was built by Sultan Shamsuddeen III for his son in 1906, becoming government property after the pair were banished in 1936. Since then it has been put to a variety of uses from the prosaic (vegetables were grown in the grounds to stave off food shortages in World War II) to the presidential (it became the head of state's official residence in 1953, although Gayoom moved out in 1994 and it now serves as his office).

*Carry on down the same road, travelling eastwards for another 100m (330ft) or so, and on your right you will see the People's Majlis (House of Parliament).*

## 7 People's Majlis

Built with money from the Pakistani government, the Maldivian Parliament is an impressively unpretentious building seating 50 MPs.

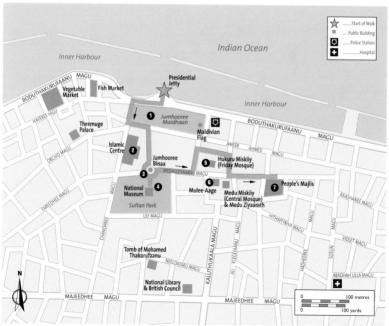

# Cowries

While today's currency of choice in the Maldives is without doubt the US dollar, the coinage of yesteryear is far more intriguing. Cowrie (or cowry) shells are marine shells found mainly in tropical regions, which were used extensively throughout much of Asia, Africa and Arabia as a means of exchange. By the 9th century, the Maldives was already an established producer.

Like much about the Maldives, the origins of the cowrie trade are obscure, but the country is believed to have been at the centre of the industry for 4,000 years. A volatile currency, cowries brought huge profits to some. Ibn Battuta, the 14th-century explorer and chronicler, reported that within one seven-year period shells sold in Male soared from between 400,000 and 1,200,000 to the dinar to 1,150 to the dinar on sale in Mali, West Africa. However, they were just as liable to plummet in value. While it is said that in the early 19th century a woman could be bought for two cowries in what is now Uganda, multiple exports over the next half century or so eroded their worth to such an extent that by 1860, 2,500 cowries were needed to buy a cow, four or five of which could be exchanged for a woman.

In the intervening centuries, the Arabs, who dominated the cowrie trade between the Maldives and East Africa in the early years, were supplanted by Europeans, first the Portuguese, then the Dutch. The shells financed the slave trade in West Africa, the peak of which, in the middle of the 18th century, brought so many cowries into circulation that their value began to drop. But they continued to be used, and held their own in East Africa, despite the region developing an indigenous cowrie industry. Part of the reason for this may have been that Maldivian cowries were smaller and lighter than their

The range of shells to be found in the Maldives

The *Cypraea moneta* is normally between 20 and 40mm (¾ and 1½in) long

East African counterparts, which meant lower transportation costs. It was not until the 1920s that the increasing use of metal coins finally sounded the death knell for the cowrie as currency and the rupee supplanted it in the region.

The cowrie trade was a notable success story for the Maldives, a place with obvious limitations on production and exportation. It did not thrive solely because the marine invertebrate *Cypraea moneta* was so numerous throughout the country, although that helped. The Maldivians also came up with an efficient method of collecting the creatures. It involved bundles of coconut palm leaves being spread out in shallow lagoons, on which the cowries would gather, feeding on the detritus that amassed on the palms. The bundles were then shifted onto the beach, where the heat of the sun would kill the invertebrates. They would then be buried, where the bodies would rot and be eaten by parasites, leaving clean shells ready for use.

Robust, difficult to forge and with a limited number available, cowries shared some of the advantages of modern coinage. While their life as currency may be over, they are still involved in Maldivian financial transactions; a pair of cowries is to be seen on every banknote.

## Artificial beach

Unsurprisingly, Male's artificial beach, on the east side of the island with big buildings looming in the background, isn't a patch on any of the resort island beaches, but as the only stretch of sand in the whole of the capital, it is very popular with Male residents. Families, joggers and young people flock there, and it sees a lot of activity in the evening. If you have time, it is worth a visit as one of the few chances the visitor gets to see ordinary Maldivian life.

## Chandanee Magu

This small shopping district at the north end of Chandanee Magu used to be known as the Singapore Bazaar, owing to the origin of many of the imports on sale there. It no longer goes by that name, but it remains the best tourist shopping area on the island with a cluster of boutiques selling souvenirs including traditional Maldivian products such as mats, as well as the standard holiday fare of T-shirts, postcards, books and art. Shopkeepers round here are highly likely to speak good English and it may be possible to bargain for goods, although this is not the norm in the Maldives. Further down the road is the part where local people shop. It may not yield as many souvenirs but it can give a rare glimpse of ordinary people going about their daily business.

## Islamic Centre

In a country characterised by low buildings designed to blend in with nature, and simplicity over ostentation, the country's largest edifice is as close

The artificial beach in Male

A view of the impressive Islamic Centre

to an exception as possible. Its golden dome is the dominant feature of the cityscape, and its glaring white walls demand attention. The huge prayer hall, which can house up to 5,000 people, is ornately decorated with Arabic writing and wood carvings. There's a marble floor on the upper level, with huge chandeliers hanging down from the high ceiling. As flagship mosques go, it has a laid-back feel, with some of the worshippers inside it actually lying around. It is also modern, built in 1984, and is bright and airy.

Guides congregate outside, hoping to latch onto the few foreign visitors – this does not remotely feel like an overrun tourist attraction – and 'show them around'. In reality, seeing the centre consists of little more than walking up the imposing front steps, standing on the viewing gallery and having a look round, and the information the guides impart (or what can be understood of it; the level of English is not universally high) is the same as that available from any guide book or website.

*Between Medhuziyaarai Magu and Ameeru Ahmed Magu. Open: daily 9am–5pm, except prayer times. Free admission.*

Waiting for customers in the fish market

## Markets

### Fish market

Given that most visitors will leave the Maldives with an impression of a country of the utmost serenity, the fish market presents a rare opportunity to see the islanders at their most active. The market is in action all day long, but gets into full swing in the afternoon, when the majority of fishing boats return with their day's catch, which is whipped off the *dhoni*, transferred to the market and prepared for sale. One of the most fascinating sights at the market is the speed and efficiency with which the vendors clean, gut and chop the fish, with one after the other being reduced from recognisable creature to anonymous meat with a few swift swishes of the knife. Another is the centrepiece catch, enormous eels, which you might glimpse when snorkelling if you're lucky, laid out in the middle of the market. While the eels are the most impressive, bonito, tuna and swordfish make up the bulk of the offerings. Upstairs is a balcony with a few shops and a small café where you can sample some of the day's catch, as fresh as it comes. You're very unlikely to be hassled, as the vendors realise that foreign visitors could do little with fresh fish and are there as tourists rather than potential customers.

The fish market is probably not an advisable stop-off for the squeamish. Naturally it has a strong smell, and the blood and guts strewn all over the floor will not be to everyone's taste. Even worse for any sensitive souls, some of the fish are still alive and flapping around in a vain struggle to avoid their fate. Ethical vegetarians and children had better be prepared.

*Between Boduthakurufaanu Magu and Haveeree Higu. Open: daily 6am–9pm approximately.*

## Vegetable market

A less potentially upsetting venue than its fishy equivalent is the vegetable market, sometimes known as the local market, further along the road to the west. While it's still busy, the atmosphere is not quite as frenetic as it is along the road. Most eye-catching is the local fruit on display, including hanging bunches of bananas, mangos, coconuts, watermelons, papayas, limes, pomegranates and screw pine. As well as the fresh fruit, stalls sell sweetmeats, nuts, oil, eggs, chillies and spices, although vegetables themselves are somewhat thinner on the ground, pretty much limited to potatoes and onions.

You may also be able to pick up some local handicrafts here. Immediately in front of the market is an area frequented by traders in firewood, underwear, watches and other market staples, another good point to observe Maldivians at work. This is the hub to which traders from various atolls come to ply their wares, so it represents a true geographical cross-section of society.

Because the traders know that here, unlike at the fish market, there is a chance tourists might make a purchase, you will be the subject of occasional sales pitches, although these are nothing as persistent as the hard sell you'd get in India or many other Asian countries. It is also possible to engage some of the stall owners in conversation.

*Between Boduthakurufaanu Magu and Haveeree Higu.*

Bananas are on sale in abundance in the vegetable market

## Mosques

Given its prominence in national life, it is little surprise that religion gives the Maldivian capital many of its places of interest. With around 20 or 30 mosques in Male, depending on whose estimate you accept, it is difficult to walk far without coming across one. Non-Muslims are usually allowed to go inside, although this may be a little intrusive during prayer time, and the places are pleasant oases of calm and quiet in a noisy city. As well as dressing modestly, covering your arms, legs and shoulders, you should remove your shoes and leave them outside; it will usually be obvious where to put them. Many mosques are surrounded by a cemetery. Graves of women are marked by round-topped stones, those of men by pointed tips. Children have smaller headstones, as do poor people. The majority of mosques are concentrated in the same part of Male that is home to all of the main highlights, so if you walk around that area you are guaranteed to pass several.

### Hukuru Miskiiy (Friday Mosque)

With its origins dating back to the 12th century, the Friday Mosque was renewed and took its current form in 1656. The country's most eminent and oldest mosque is also one of its most visually impressive. Coral curving, beautifully carved panelling, original timber and much other evidence of traditional workmanship are just some of the fascinating features worth seeing. Unlike many buildings of its kind, the mosque is more impressive from the inside than the outside. Non-Muslims

Hukuru Miskiiy, the Friday Mosque, is protected by an ugly tin roof

مسجد السلطان محمد بن عبد الله

Detail on a mosque in Male

are allowed to go in, but permission must be sought from the Supreme Council of Islamic Affairs. The mosque spent four centuries as its country's main place of worship, however, the construction of the Islamic Centre and its Grand Friday Mosque usurped it in 1984.
*Between Medhuziyaarai Magu and Ameeru Ahmed Magu.*

### Idu Miskiiy (Eid Mosque)

One of the highest ranked mosques in terms of religious significance, the Eid Mosque was rebuilt at the start of the 19th century. The old stone pulpit is still visible, although it is no longer in use. In past times, the mosque was frequented by sultans celebrating the Eid-ul-Fitr and Eid-ul-Adha festivals. Parts of the design betray Buddhist influence.
*Hadhuvaru Magu.*

### Medu Miskiiy (Central Mosque)

Particular sacredness is conferred on this mosque by the burial plot to which it is attached, the blue and white Medu Ziyaarath (Central Shrine), resting place of Abu al-Barakat al-Barbari, the Moroccan who is credited with converting the kingdom to Islam in 1153. The site was considered so holy that the sultan was only allowed to enter it on seven days of the year. The mosque has long been considered one of the most attractive on the island.
*Medhuziyaarai Magu.*

A guide stands by a model of a traditional house in the National Museum

## National Museum

Given that the Maldives' resort islands are rather bereft of local culture, apart from the most sanitised kind, and that the government does its utmost to try to deter visitors from visiting the places where genuine Maldivian life is lived, the museum offers a wonderful chance for a foreigner to get acquainted with the country's history and culture. It is housed in what remains of the Sultan's Palace, a three-storey colonial-style building that still retains original features such as the handwritten Koran text engraved on the walls. The atmosphere has much in common with other museums throughout the subcontinent, a somewhat ad hoc arrangement of exhibits, the musty atmosphere of an old warehouse, and men selling tickets who seem as old as some of the artefacts.

The items on show run the gamut from the pre-Islamic period to modern times. Buddhist culture is represented by sandstone and coral pieces said to be remnants of temples found in the 11th century, as well as coral Buddha heads. The colourful lives of the Maldivian nobles are another source of fascinating items, such as sumptuous thrones, a remarkable palanquin (a conveyance borne by four servants), costumes, turbans, armour and other sultan paraphernalia. The exhibits also chronicle the history of the Maldives, including the first printing press to be used in the country, bullet-riven motorbikes from failed coups, weapons and a Maldivian flag that was taken to the moon by NASA.

Objects can be viewed from close up, although you may be followed around by a museum worker to check that you don't touch anything. With so many interesting artefacts, the museum clearly has a space problem, with some objects stacked outside. The Maldivian Centre for Linguistic and Historical Research intends to expand the collection, and the extension of the museum is under consideration. *Sultan Park. Tel: 332 2254. Open: Sat–Thur 8am–6pm, Fri 4–6pm. Closed: government holidays. Admission charge.*

A Sultan's throne on display in the National Museum

## Sultan Park

The park that is home to the Sultan's Palace is the southern, oldest part and all that remains of the old Sultan's Palace and its grounds, after the palace was largely demolished in 1968, having fallen into disrepair (although some argue that more of it could have been saved). The site dates back to the 17th century. An informal division seems to have sprung up between Male's main two green spaces. While local people dominate Jumhooree Maidhaan, sitting around in the shade and watching the world go by, Sultan Park seems to be the preserve mainly of foreign workers, plus the tourists for whom it is a regular stop on the standard Male tour organised by resorts. It is certainly a

### ANDREAS ANDRE

Despite being born locally and brought up Muslim, Andreas Andre ruled the country as Portuguese regent during the 15-year occupation. The mother of Andiri Andirin, as the Maldivians knew him, was a sister of the king of Goa. On an exploratory trip to the Maldives, while pregnant with Andreas, she witnessed her husband's death at the hands of warrior Black Ibrahim, and she agreed to convert to Islam and marry him rather than suffer the same fate. Andreas later fled to Goa after murdering his half-brother, and returned with the Portuguese fleet to take Male in 1558. Until as recently as the 1950s, the invader was strangely commemorated with a street in Male bearing his name.

pleasant place for a sit down or a stroll, with its neat pathways and orderly botanical displays of brightly coloured

The entrance to pretty Sultan Park

The new presidential palace is quite similar to the previous one (*see p13*)

tropical flora. The park's busiest time is on Friday afternoons, when it has reduced opening hours. Access is through the impressive wrought-iron gates.

The southeast corner of the park is home to one of the city's most well-travelled mosques which is said to have been transferred, in small pieces, to Bandos island, where it was reassembled, following which the decision was made to bring it back to the capital, whereupon the whole process was reversed.

*Between Medhuziyaarai Magu,*
*Chandanee Magu and Lily Magu.*
*Open: Sat–Thur 8am–6pm, Fri 4–6pm.*
*Free admission.*

## Theemuge

The new Presidential Palace, designed by a Malaysian architect, has only recently reached completion. With its blue and white aesthetic, it is not dissimilar from its predecessor Mulee-Aage, although it is larger and grander-looking. It sits in an enclave of state buildings including the Ministry of Justice and Islamic Affairs and Hilaaleege, the government guesthouse. Its architecture is somewhat eclectic, combining local motifs with more modern elements. The president hosts receptions in Theemuge and on special occasions deigns to meet some of his people there.

*Orchid Magu.*

# Atoll formation

The Maldives is so closely associated with atoll formation that even the word itself is said to have Dhivehi origins, a derivation of *atholhu*. The process fascinated scientists including the 19th-century scientist and writer Charles Darwin. While he never made it to the Maldives in person, he studied maps of the area extensively and read up on it, and subsequently came up with a theory of atoll formation in 1842.

The English naturalist thought the prevailing idea of the time – that an atoll was the coral-coated rim of a volcano crater – was wrong. He posited that the atoll was formed through a process of subsidence when a small volcanic island or mountain peak sank into the sea. Now accepted as basically correct, at the time Darwin's theory was revolutionary.

His thinking was that the different kinds of tropical island (volcanic, barrier reef and atoll) were at different stages of subsidence from the starting point of an ocean volcano. Coral would grow in the warm, shallow waters around the island, keeping up with the sea level as it rose (or the island as it sank). Biotic growth (caused by organisms) would keep the outer part of the reef close to sea level, while the inside part, facing tougher conditions, would lag behind and slowly become a lagoon. The volcano would eventually sink beneath the surface of the water, leaving only the barrier reef or a ring of small islands; an atoll. Without the organisms, the process would be impossible, which is why atolls could only form in waters of a certain temperature, and ocean islands situated in warm enough areas are now described as being at Darwin Point, in recognition of the naturalist's discoveries.

However, his theory has not gone unchallenged. Canadian geologist Reginald Aldworth Daly believed that islands worn down by erosion during a glacial stand became atolls as the water level was pushed upwards by melting glaciers. While the fluctuation of the sea level looks certain to have been a contributory factor in atoll development, further discoveries seem to support Darwin's view. Darwin wrote to the American oceanographer Alexander Agassiz, 'I wish some doubly rich millionaire would take it into his head to have borings made in some of the Pacific and Indian atolls, and bring home

The Maldives comprises 22 atolls composed of almost 1,200 islets

cores for slicing from a depth of 400 to 600 feet.' When this drilling did take place – although over ten times deeper than Darwin had envisaged – his theory was confirmed.

The Maldives consists of 22 atolls plus some smaller islands that can be described as smaller atoll formations, with broad and deep channels running between them. All of the country's above-sea land is of coralline origin. While this unique geography and the atolls' neat configuration make for a marvellous bird's eye view, they were not so appreciated by early navigators, for whom charting them was a perilous undertaking. Robert Moresby, a British Royal Navy captain and maritime surveyor, attempted the cartography of the country in 1834–6. Although not perfect, the resulting maps were held in such high regard that they were personally inspected by Queen Victoria and helped Maldivian sailors navigate the atolls up until they were replaced by satellite maps in the 1990s.

# North Male Atoll

*With Male having been the centre of national life for as long as records date back, much of its development, both local and touristic, is centred on the North Male Atoll. Some 50km (31 miles) long, it is home to around 10,000 Maldivians (excluding the capital). It is home to the earliest tourist resorts in the country. Kurumba first opened its doors in October 1972, followed two months later by Bandos (previously an orphanage). The resorts in this area are therefore the most established, and also the most numerous.*

While it would be misleading to suggest that anywhere in the Maldives could be considered a party destination, this atoll is home to what night-time action there is, owing in large part to the regular presence of airline crews in some of the larger resorts, enjoying their stopover between flights. Local industry is also active here. Thulusdhoo has a Coca-Cola bottling plant that uses desalinated water, as the Maldivians are keen to tell foreign visitors. The island also has a large warehouse for dried fish, which is so plentiful that it is occasionally used to fill pot-holes in the road. None of this activity will impinge on your holiday in the slightest. The waters are as pristine in the atoll as they are anywhere else.

Because of the impossibility of designating one island more important than any other, they are listed throughout this guide in alphabetical order.

### Angsana

Angsana's top attraction is probably its house reef, widely regarded as the best in the atoll, if not the entire country. The encircling reef is handy for snorkellers, just a couple of metres from the shore, and its steep incline is home to a huge variety of fish. Divers have a wealth of sites within a short

A heron fishes from the jetty in Angsana

distance of the island. There are plenty of other water sports available, and experienced participants are given the freedom to go off independently. The other way to pass the time is in the island's super spa, where Thai and Indonesian therapists cater to guests in eight treatment rooms. There is also a gallery, a CD and book library and a well-stocked gift shop with largely imported items.

Having operated as a resort since 1979, in 2001 the site was taken over by the Banyan Tree, which also runs the adjacent island facility. Angsana is more laid back than its neighbour, decorated with bright, bold colours rather than the more muted tones of its sister resort, and quirky touches such as real apples feature in the interior design. As next door, there are no TV sets in the rooms, although children are permitted.

Angsana shares with Banyan Tree its focus on preserving the environment, and some parts of the small, oval island are off-limits to visitors for that reason.

Its eco-friendly projects include reef cleaning, turtle breeding, sandbagging and barnacle building, and its efforts have seen it claim several environmental awards. The thatched accommodation, 45 villas in two categories, is in keeping with the natural, relaxed vibe beloved of independent travellers, and with its verdant foliage, which has contributed to its status as the most photographed island in the Maldives. A small island, it is located away from the rim, in the southern half of the atoll.

*Tel: 664 0326. Email: maldives@ angsana.com. www.angsana.com*

## Bandos

The second island to be given over to tourism, Bandos provided accommodation of a different kind in the 1960s – as an orphanage. It is one of the livelier islands. Being large and so close to Male it is the resort of choice for several airlines. Not only is it subsequently populated by cabin crews, but it is also a stop-off on island-hopping tours and gets day-trippers from the capital. Evenings here may see guests entertained by Maldivian calypso bands or *Bodu Beru* dancers. But while Bandos is fairly dynamic by sleepy Maldivian standards, there are places to find some peace. The island's attractive beaches come with plenty of vegetation, creating small patches of privacy where you can forget you're on a relatively large island.

The resort's diving facilities are particularly good; the island has one of the country's few decompression chambers. The house reef, some 40–60m (130–200ft) from the shoreline, is also very well regarded.

Interesting shapes of roofs in Bandos

Water villas extending out over the sea in North Male Atoll

Bandos is in the middle of the atoll, to the south.
*Tel: 664 0088. Email: sales@ bandos.com.mv. www.bandos.com.mv*

### Banyan Tree

Formerly operating as Vabbinfaru from 1977, the Banyan Tree chain took over the place in 1995. With its emphasis on eco-friendliness, the resort manages to combine the concepts of high luxury and harmony with nature seamlessly. An on-site marine biologist oversees various projects to protect the local environment and wildlife, including turtles, sharks and coral, with occasional help from visiting top scientists in their field. Guests and members of staff are encouraged to get involved with activities like the house reef cleans, and anyone interested in finding out more can pop along to the office for lessons. Some good snorkelling is possible by the house reef, and there are daily events involving the turtles and stingrays, which are fed from near the jetty.

The atmosphere of the island is relaxed, with no television sets in the rooms and no children under the age of 12 admitted to the resort. Accommodation is in individually designed villas in the shape of seashells, with thatched roofs that add to the atmosphere of natural simplicity. With only 48 villas on the island, there is plenty of privacy, which is enhanced by the coconut palms and bougainvillea shrubs. As well as a well-equipped diving and water-sports centre, the other main way to pass the time is in the spa, where Thai masseuses administer a variety of treatments in the five pavilions.

Tel: 664 3147. Email: maldives@
banyantree.com. www.banyantree.com

## Baros

Another of the groups of resorts that
have been operating since the early
1970s, Baros, which opened hot on the
heels of the early birds in 1973, is a
smaller and more intimate resort, with
upmarket villa-style accommodation.
The semicircular island gets a lot of
repeat customers and honeymooners,
who enjoy the privacy afforded by the
dense vegetation, teeming with hibiscus
and bougainvillea. Much of the
shoreline is decent beach. For ocean-
based activity, the house reef is close by
and easily accessible thanks to the
lagoon configuration, there is good
snorkelling and the diving school is also
well run. Baros is in the cluster of
central, southern islands in the atoll.
Tel: 664 2672. Email: reservations@
baros.com.mv. www.baros.com

## Full Moon

Full Moon was converted from
Furanafushi and has been operational
since 1993. It is a relatively large island
and much of its shoreline is high-
quality beach. Somewhat unusually
for the Maldives, some of the
accommodation is in two-storey
buildings, but the thatched roofs give
the place more of a village feel. Like
many of the bigger resorts, Full Moon
provides a full entertainment
programme, including nightly events,
and has a piano bar with karaoke.

It has six different restaurants and a
spa. There are also tennis courts,
a gym and an outdoor whirlpool, and
windsurfing is among the water
sports on offer.

The diving school has access to a
large lagoon. Full Moon is also the
nearest island to Banana Reef, a 300m
(330yd) dive site so named because its
shape resembles the fruit. The reef was
one of the first diving sites to be
discovered and developed owing to its
proximity to the capital, and remains
one of the country's top locations for
divers. A section of the reef has broken
away, and there are canyons, caves and
overhangs to explore. Fish that inhabit
the area include bluelined snappers,
moray eels, angelfish, bannerfish,
coral hinds, long-jawed squirrelfish
and giant groupers. The area does
experience strong currents. Full Moon
lies to the south of the atoll, on the
eastern rim.
Tel: 664 2010. Email: reservations@
fullmoon.com.mv.
www.fullmoonmaldives.com

## Giravaru

While most infrastructure and facilities
in the Maldives seem – and probably
were – purposely designed to prevent
independent travellers from
spontaneous exploration of the
country, Giravaru is an exception.
It still gets fully occupied, but it can
sometimes be possible to call ahead and
book in for a few days. Just west of
Male, and the closest resort island in

that direction, it is also well placed geographically for a spur-of-the-moment visit. Independent types will also enjoy the atmosphere. As one of the few resorts in the country that are privately run, it doesn't have the corporate chain identity of some of the more upmarket hotels.

The island holds an important place in Maldivian history. Its former residents (who were moved out to make way for the resort) claim to be descended from the country's earliest settlers, Dravidian people from the Indian subcontinent and modern-day Sri Lanka. The place is on the small side, with just two decent beaches, but its greatest asset is its water sports opportunities. With an impressive reef and plenty of fish visible a few metres away from the jetty, beginners can snorkel without fear, and the lagoon to the west of the island is also suited to snorkelling as well as windsurfers learning the ropes.

More challenging is the scuba-diving in the vicinity. The Vadhoo Channel is considered one of the top diving sites in the world. Kuda Haa, a protected area, has two *thilas* (coral-covered structures that protrude from the water) and a huge diversity of fish including dogtooth tuna, feather stars, scorpion fish, lionfish, moray eels, butterfly fish, sea squirts, and leaf fish. Sharks are also a common sight, as they are at Lion's Head. There, overhangs and caves are home to soldier-fish, lobsters and groupers. Octopuses, turtles, pipefish and stonefish can also be spotted, although the oil and gas facilities in the background are a less welcome sight. Hans Hass Place is another protected area in the vicinity hosting a wide variety of creatures. Giravaru's dive centre **Planeta Divers** is highly reputed (*www.planetadivers.com*). Note that from August 2007 the resort closed for renovations. Check its website (*www.giravaru.com*) for re-opening details.

Meeru Island, with its villas hidden among the trees

*Tel: 664 0440. Email: giravaru@ dhivehinet.net.mv. www.giravaru.com*

## Kurumba

The oldest resort in the Maldives, Kurumba has a chequered history. Mohamed Amin Didi, the country's first president, was imprisoned on the island (known at the time as Vihamanaafushu) after being overthrown in a coup in 1953. He died there after a stay of several months. Over a half century later, it is difficult to conceive of the island as a prison. It is a verdant site, blooming with bougainvillea, frangipani shrubs and palm trees. Other natural attractions include the coral formations at the Feydhoo Caves, a top dive site. The house reef also lays claim to impressive coral and a thousand different kinds of fauna. The island's resident diving company is the Swiss firm **Euro Divers**, which is popular among expatriates in Male.

While the island, as the grand dame of Maldivian resorts, has something of a tradition in hospitality, it has also been quick to embrace the modern. Despite its size – just 0.8km ($^1/_2$ mile) long – electric cars are used to transport guests to their accommodation. There is also a shopping centre, conference hall and business centre, and the resort's proximity to Male, just ten minutes by speedboat, makes it suitable for pressed-for-time business people.
*Euro Divers. www.euro-divers.com. Tel: 664 2324. Email: kurumba@ dhivehi.net.mv. www.universalresorts.com*

## Meeru

Meeru is another of the largest islands in North Male Atoll. You can walk around it in approximately 45 minutes. It is fairly remote from all other resort islands, apart from Asdu Sun. It is an attractive place, where the already abundant greenery has mostly been left alone to flourish. The proximity of more than 50 underwater sites brings a lot of divers to the island, with large fish, tuna, barracudas, manta rays and sharks visible at sites that range from easy to very difficult. Dhiffushi, an inhabited island, is also nearby. Meeru

Dive down to see fish among wrecks at Meeru

Paradise Island beach lives up to its name

is midway between the top and bottom of the atoll, at its easternmost point.

## Paradise Island

The island's long narrow shape, one kilometre (²/₃ mile) long, delivers a surfeit of pleasant beach, which never gets crowded, despite the relatively high number of rooms, and there is a great deal of greenery. Much of this was integrated by the owners, and the nursery is said to hold 10,000 plants.

The resort plays host to airline crew, part of the reason why it is one of the 'party' islands (used in the loosest possible, Maldives sense). There's a dedicated karaoke room, and regular evening entertainment, including live bands and crab racing. Presumably this is a far cry from the island's first incarnation as the simpler resort of

Lankanfinolhu. Other activities include a gamut of sports both in the water and on land. Windsurfing, waterskiing, jet skiing, catamaran sailing, parasailing and canoeing are all possibilities, and the PADI accredited diving centre is run by a friendly and helpful staff. On dry land guests can choose from tennis, squash, badminton, volleyball, basketball, table tennis and snooker, and there is also a gym. The large capacity also allows the hotel to cater to business groups, and there is a conference hall and committee rooms. Paradise is on the eastern rim of the atoll.
*Tel: 664 0011. Email: info@paradise-island.com.mv. www.villahotels.com*

## Soneva Gili

Advertising itself as the first resort to offer exclusively water-villa-based

accommodation, Soneva Gili was formerly known as Lankanfushi, and is in the south east of the atoll. There are 44 separate rooms, and the relatively small number keeps the emphasis on romance and solitude rather than partying and activity. 'Doing' something here usually means going to the spa, a Six Senses outlet with glass floor panels that allow you to fish spot while the therapist gets to work on kneading away your stress. The resort is another that tries to balance the often conflicting concepts of lavishness and environmental friendliness; rooms come with quadraphonic hi-fi, television and video compact disc but they are stashed away in a handmade wooden cabinet so as not to spoil the authentic Maldivian feel. Accommodation has been built with each unit at a discrete distance from its neighbours, to help prevent the place feeling even a tiny bit busy. However, if even this is not privacy enough, reclusive guests can opt for one of the seven Crusoe residences that are so separate that you need a rowing boat to get there from the jetty. The resort is one of the 'no news, no shoes' subscribers; however, this simplicity does not extend to the dining options, which are sophisticated. There is plenty of opportunity to take romantic meals for two in a venue of your choice, including on a desert island.
*Tel: 664 0304. Email: reservations-gili@ sonevaresorts.com. www.sixsenses.com*

## A PRESIDENTIAL DILEMMA

The Maldivian government's attempts to keep foreign tourists (with their drinking, scanty clothing and other un-Islamic proclivities) apart from the conservative Muslim population, while simultaneously encouraging tourism for the dollars it generates, are undoubtedly testing moral ground. And the opposition group, the Maldivian Democratic Party, were quick to condemn apparent hypocrisy from President Gayoom in March 2007 over a foreigner's decadent, resort-based birthday party. British tycoon Sir Philip Green had topless dancing, an 11m (36ft) Buddha and copious champagne at the celebrity bash. But far from censuring the excess, Gayoom personally called Green to thank him for choosing the Maldives to celebrate and wished him a happy birthday.

## Thulhaagiri

With a simple, village aesthetic, Thulhaagiri is one of the island resorts that truly adhere to the 'back to nature' concept. This is encapsulated by the thatched roofs on much of the accommodation and the extensive use of wood in the rooms and water bungalows. A small, coral island, with a maximum occupancy of 144, it's possible to walk around the whole place in little over ten minutes. Copious bushes and plants add to the feeling of privacy. Trees in the area outside the reception, which has a small pond, contain birdhouses for over 150 brilliantly coloured parrots. The resort managers also take care to ensure the house reef is protected, by asking guests not to walk on it.

Thulhaagiri water villas blend in with their surroundings

While some parts of the reef offer decent snorkelling, the island is also near enough to other reefs and dive sites to satisfy water-sports enthusiasts. The island sits in a big lagoon used for swimming and boating, as well as windsurfing and waterskiing. Everything you might need for diving or other water sports is provided by the dive centre. The underdeveloped feel and the fact that the resort managers have made a deliberate decision not to upgrade the hotel into an already crowded higher category ensure plenty of repeat visitors. The island is in the centre and to the south of the North Male Atoll.

*Tel: 664 5930. Email: reserve@ thulhaagiri.com.mv. www.thulhaagiri.com*

# Walk: Villingili

*Once a resort, that closed in 1990, Villingili is now used as a village island to cope with the overflow from Male, lying about 2km (1¼ miles) to the east. No permit is required to visit it so it is one of the easiest ways to see Maldivian life outside the capital. Being so close to the capital, Villingili has taken on some of Male's characteristics, but it has a far more serene pace of life and makes a great escape from the hustle and bustle over the water.*

*To get to Villingili, take the ferry from the New Harbour terminal at the southwest corner of Male. The journey takes no more than about 15 minutes and ferries depart every half an hour. Tickets, which cost Rf3 one-way, are on sale from a small kiosk at the terminal. A relatively small island, about 800m × 600m (½ mile × ³⁄₈ mile), much of it can be seen in an hour.*

*Start at the ferry terminal where you will arrive. Take an immediate left and walk south to the beach.*

## 1 The beach

The beach here is gorgeous, with plenty of shade thanks to the beautiful big, old trees, some of which seem to be growing at impossibly horizontal angles. The area is popular with local families and children, surfers and independent travellers looking for a change from the package holiday atmosphere. It also provides an unusual view of Male.

*Continue along the beach until you can go no further. At that point, rejoin the road and continue in the same direction until you get to a right turn. Take it and follow the road for 50m (160ft) or so. On your right you will see a Teacher Centre and then the local school.*

## 2 Villingili School

Go in school hours and the compound is alive with children dashing about in the courtyard. It's another cheering peek at local life on the islands.

*Take the road directly south of the school (left of the direction from which you approached) and follow the road round as it bears to the right. You will reach another pleasant beach area. As the beach begins to narrow and the shoreline begins to go north, you will see the Old Mosque.*

## 3 Old Mosque

Interesting old structure that provides a striking counterpart to the spanking new mosque on the other side of the football pitch.

*Take the road to the east of the mosque and head north. After around 150m (¹/₈ mile) you will come to the football pitch on your right.*

## 4 Football pitch

Earmarked to be turned into a stadium, it's only of interest if you're lucky enough to catch a game in action. There's a small café in the southwest corner.

*Keep following the road to the left of the football pitch northwards. On your left you'll see the new mosque.*

## 5 Villingili Mosque

Masjidhul Ikhlaas, or the Villingili Mosque, is a pretty building funded by local entrepreneur Ismail Ibrahim and opened by the president himself.

*From the mosque either go right along the road opposite the mosque, which will lead you back to the ferry terminal, or, for a more leisurely return, continue along the road you were on until you reach the harbour. You can then follow the sea road back to your starting point.*

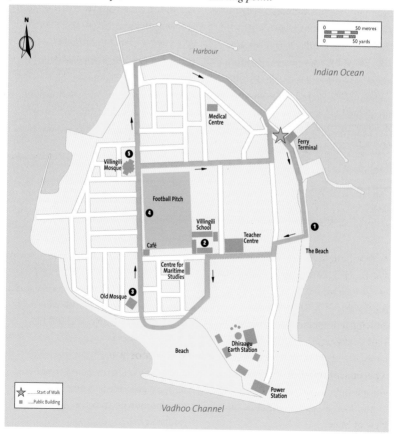

# Black magic

Given the strict adherence to Islam insisted upon by the Maldives' theocratic regime, the country's belief in demons, spirits and black and white magic seems at best inconsistent and at worse sacrilegious. However, the other salient aspects of the country – the treacherous sea and submerged coral reefs that sent many ancient mariners to a watery grave, deserted islands of which little was known and a country isolated from most external communication and media – provided fertile ground for such a belief system to take hold.

Even the story said to explain the country's initial conversion to Islam (*see panel p141*) is a mythological one, with its demon and sacrificial virgins. The faith allows for a belief in *jinni*, or genies, supernatural creatures made of fire, visible only to a select few, who can communicate with them. Such people were called on to perform an exorcism when a *jinni* possessed someone. But the credence of the spirit world went further than that, such that the belief was generally hidden from outsiders, with Maldivian Muslims fearful of seeming un-Islamic.

The mysticism of the islands seems to have two branches. *Fandita* refers to traditional alternative health practices, white magic and astrology, and mostly takes the form of lucky charms, harmless concoctions and incantations. Its aim is to ensure luck, love or wealth, and it is quite legal. It is commonly used to confer luck on a new boat at its launch or when harvesting crops. *Sihuru* is more malevolent – and illegal. Practitioners could get a hefty punishment if caught. It is used to physically harm people, sending them mad or ill. *Sihuru* spells can be effected through administering food to the victim or burying something like a coconut or a black charm.

Some islands in the Maldives were thought to be haunted. When the spirits, or *dhevi*, cause problems, the local ghostbusters are the *fanditavaria*, the shamans who can see and communicate with the apparitions. The spirits take various forms and various levels of malevolence. One of the worst is the *vigani*, the ancient lord of death. It kills and eats people, and loves putrefaction. Its terrifying presence is signified by a one-coloured rainbow. Another undesirable spirit is the *handi*, a fair woman distinguishable by her long, messy hair and red

Some spirits are still believed to have murderous powers here

costume. If disturbed, she is believed to be able to travel very fast and drive her victims mad. The *baburu kujjaa*, one of the most common demons, has the appearance of a child, and comes out at night to haunt people. A *fureytha* smells bad and has eyes on the top of its head.

Not all of the spirits are so ghastly. A shape-shifting *avahtehi*, despite her unkempt appearance, is an invisible being who – very handily – can be trained to do the housework, and also befriends people. And a *kandumathi elhun*, who affects boats, can even speed up a vessel, if it appears from behind it. It can take many forms, from a ball of light, a lamp-lit ship, a salty rain shower or reef, to a dead body.

# South Male Atoll

*South Male Atoll saw the second wave of tourism development after its northern neighbour in the late 1970s. It's not as built up (as much as the Maldives can ever be said to be built up) as North Male, but is just as abundant in terms of dive sites, most of which are in the southern half of the atoll along with the majority of the resort islands.*

The atoll is slightly further from the airport island of Hulhule than its northern counterpart, and to get there you must traverse the Vadhoo Channel, the strip of ocean that divides the North and South Male Atolls; great for divers, not so great for luggage-laden boat journeys when the sea's rough. Less than half the size of its northern neighbour, the atoll is home to just 1,500 people living on three islands: Gulhi, whose inhabitants earn their living from a private shipyard; fishing village Maafushi; and Guraidhoo, home to several souvenir shops. There are 11 uninhabited islands and 17 resorts, most of which are grouped on the atoll's eastern rim.

## Bolifushi

A traditional resort, beach rooms here are fashioned from coral, wood and thatch, underlining the island's homespun ethos. Bolifushi is a little, friendly resort, which likes to keep things relaxed. The beach is generally decent, and there's no shortage of greenery. There is an entertainment programme but if you prefer a party atmosphere this is not the place to find it.

The island is in proximity to a sizeable sandbar, facilitating good catamaraning and windsurfing. There are diving opportunities, including a small wreck, but be wary of the currents to the west. The house reef is highly rated and close by, ideal for snorkelling, particularly for beginners. Bolifushi is in the northwest of the atoll, not far from Male.
*Tel: 664 3517. Email: gateway@ dhivehinet.net.mv. www.bolifushi.com*

## Club Rannalhi

The key word here is 'club'. Rannalhi is a fun island resort, with 116 rooms, lots of entertainment at night and an emphasis on joining in. This seems to appeal particularly to Italians, who make up the bulk of the clientele. A fine, albeit narrow, beach borders the island, and palms ensure plenty of shade. Some of the accommodation is in two-storey structures. The resort has been operating here since 1996, when it was shifted from a neighbouring isle. The lagoon is wide, and there is a diving school providing the usual range of water sports. Club Rannalhi is the westernmost resort in the atoll.

*Tel: 664 2688. Email: reserve@ rannalhi.com.mv. www.clubrannalhi.com*

## Cocoa Island Resort

The resort is on Makunufushi Island, a long, thin strip with plenty of plants, trees and shade and a 1-km ($^5$/$_8$-mile) sandbank. Following several overhauls it is now a very contemporary facility but draws on aspects of classic Maldivian architecture and design, for example the heavy use of wood in the construction of the rooms, including some wooden whirlpools. Like the Shambhala Spa (*see p152*), this resort is unusual in that it has yoga facilities,

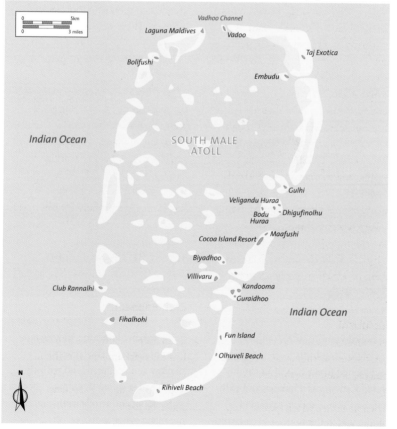

Vadhoo Channel

Laguna Maldives — Vadoo

Taj Exotica

Bolifushi

Embudu

Indian Ocean

SOUTH MALE ATOLL

Gulhi

Veligandu Huraa

Bodu Huraa — Dhigufinolhu

Cocoa Island Resort — Maafushi

Biyadhoo

Villivaru

Club Rannalhi

Kandooma

Guraidhoo

Indian Ocean

Fihalhohi

Fun Island

Olhuveli Beach

Rihiveli Beach

N

Sunset over South Male Atoll

something more common in neighbouring India.

Situated to the east of the highly rated Kandooma Channel, and with Cocoa Corner and its caves and undercuts to the south, Cocoa Island has good diving nearby, as well as a great house reef. The lagoon is shallow and sheltered, and with its sandy bed is suited to sailing, waterskiing and windsurfing, among the many water sports on offer. The resort lies halfway down the east side of South Male Atoll.

*Tel: 664 1818. Email: res@ cocoaisland.com.bz. www.cocoaisland.com.bz*

## Embudu

Embudu, which you may also see written as Embudhu or Embudhoo, is a pretty island with an attractive, if rather small in parts, beach. There is plenty of greenery and shade, and the resort is run by a friendly and down-to-earth team, with the sand floors of the lobby and reception indicative of the relaxed, barefoot ambience.

The island is well placed for a lot of high-quality diving, with access to the huge channel close by. The Embudu Kandu Marine Area, one of the dive sites in the vicinity, offers the famous drift dive known as the Embudu Express, where divers are swept along in the current past a plethora of great fish, rays and sharks. There are also the coral gardens of the Embudu Thila, Fusilier Reef to the north and a shark-viewing point. The lagoon in which Embudu is situated is a large one, and excellent snorkelling is to be had at the house reef, ideal for beginners owing to its close proximity to the island. Water sports at the resort are provided by **Diverland** (*www.diverland.com*). Embudu is on the eastern side of the atoll, close to the top.

*Tel: 664 4776. Email: embvil@ dhivehinet.net.mv. www.embudu.com*

## Fihalhohi Tourist Resort

This family-oriented, good-value resort, which has been going since 1981, is a large island, also called Lhohi Faru, rich in bird life and foliage, with tall palms providing cover. Beginners and younger tourists are well catered for in the water; the house reef is an ideal site for learning to snorkel or dive. More advanced divers will also find satisfying territory nearby, and the island offers other water sports too. Fihalhohi is at the furthest point southwest of the atoll.

*Tel: 664 2903. Email: filha@ dhivehinet.net.mv. www.filhahohi.net*

## Laguna Maldives

Laguna was one of the early-comers to the zone south of the capital, opening in 1974, but underwent a big transformation in 1991. Flecked with palm trees, it takes upwards of ten minutes to circumnavigate, which can be done, uninterrupted, on the beach, a more diverse stretch of sand than is

### REDHIN

Legend has it that the names of the Maldivian islands were given by the Redhin, a people that some believe were Dravidian migrants from southern India. Their main legacy was their architecture. Ruins attributed to Redhin religious structures have been found throughout the archipelago, evidence of their skill in masonry. Astronomy was another of their specialties. They used the planets to predict the future and worshipped the sun and fire. Generally peaceable, their religious rituals were violent. Surprisingly, given the Maldivians' appearance, they are said to have been big, light-skinned and long-nosed.

common at resorts. Laguna has legions of fans and is considered by some to be among the most beautiful islands in the country. Some of the accommodation is provided in blocks.

As well as a highly rated spa facility, on-land diversions take the form of a children's pool, tennis, a gym and a games room. If you want to get wet, there are diving and windsurfing centres, and you can also go parasailing. Novice scuba-divers can opt for a beginners' course, while old hands can get stuck in straight away at the nearby Vadhoo Channel, which intersects North and South Male Atolls, a top diving site that is ranked among the best the Maldives has to offer. Laguna sits at the top of the atoll, close to Male and Vadoo. *Tel: 664 5903. Email: lbn@dhivehinet. net.mv. www.universalresorts.com*

### Rihiveli Beach

Coming with a surfeit of names, the island (Rihiveli means silver sands) is also known as Mahaana Elhi Huraa (its original name), as well as Fenboahuraa. It's a green, shady resort with plenty of palm trees providing respite from the sun. There are two uninhabited islands in its large lagoon, whose shallowness and sandy base lend it to water sports. The resort offers windsurfing, waterskiing, canoeing, catamaraning and diving – some of which are free of charge – although snorkellers must take an organised trip as there is no house reef. The highly rated dive school runs PADI courses.

On land, it is a rustic resort (rooms come without television and air-conditioning). As well as the beach, there's a long sandbar. The evenings bring yoga and aerobics classes and local performances of dance and drumming. Rihiveli is the southernmost resort in the atoll. *Tel: 664 1994. Email: reservations@ rihiveli-maldives.com. www.rihiveli-maldives.com*

### Taj Exotica

The island's previous incarnation as the rustic Embudhu Finolhu changed considerably when it was taken over by the upmarket Taj Group. By resort standards it is medium sized, at around 800m ($1/2$ mile) long, with the villas separated by one path through the middle. The company has attempted to marry luxury and nature. The palm-thatched villas were designed with environmental impact in mind, and rely heavily on natural materials, for example in the wooden floors. The spa is run by the Indonesian company Mandara, and unlike at other hotels, there are no buffets or fixed meal times.

Weak swimmers will enjoy the safe conditions of the island's location in the middle of a large, sandy lagoon – one of the biggest in the country. Delphis Dive and Water Sports Centre is PADI-recognised and also offers catamaraning, windsurfing, canoeing and parasailing. The absence of a house reef means guests must be taken to a platform over the coral ridge. Taj is on

One of the tree-fringed beaches on Club Rannalhi resort island

the eastern rim of South Male Atoll at the northern end, and one of the closest resorts to Male.
*Tel: 664 2200. Email: exotica.maldives@ tajhotels.com. www.tajhotels.com*

### Vadoo

The fact that the resort originally operated under the name Vadoo Diving Paradise gives a good indication of its chief asset. Located close to Male, Vadoo lies right on the channel that shares its name (albeit spelt slightly differently) and over a dozen of the best diving sites in the country are within easy reach, five of which are designated marine areas. The channel, which divides the North and South Male Atolls, ensures a huge diversity of sea creatures are present, and you have a good chance of spotting dolphins, sharks, eagle and manta rays plus a plethora of reef fish. Instructors at the diving centre provide both NAUI and PADI courses. There are strong currents to be wary of, but the house reef is also highly reputed, and catamaraning, waterskiing and snorkelling are also available.

The island itself and its beaches are lush and small; you can do a circuit in about five minutes. Thatched roofs and pine décor add to the natural style, with marble adding a touch of luxury. The size of the place limits the number of guests, which in turn rules out much chance of any nightlife. Vadoo is not the place to come if you want to party.
*Tel: 664 3976. Email: vadoo@ vadoo.com.mv. www.vadoo.net*

# Tour: Island-hopping

*With the Maldivian government doing its level best to isolate tourists from locals and ensure that never the twain shall meet, thwarted efforts to get to know the local culture can be one of the few frustrations of an otherwise perfect holiday. Whereas trips to neighbouring destinations such as India and Sri Lanka present the traveller with unlimited opportunities to mix, unchaperoned, with local people and participate in local life, the logistics and bureaucracy of the Maldives render this almost impossible.*

To visit a village island generally requires an Inter Atoll Travel Permit issued by the Ministry of Atolls Administration in Male, and your application must be supported by a resident of the island you wish to see – the more prominent and influential the better. Few have the contacts, time or inclination to pursue this on a two-week trip. Even if your intentions are as modest as visiting another resort island, things can get messy and expensive, with the required permission to dock, docking fees and resort charges all standing in the way of spontaneous day trips. This is where your hotel can help. On an island-hopping trip, no permits are needed, as you are in the 'custody' of the staff. Most islands offer this kind of excursion, usually for a half or full day, and all take a similar form.

### Deserted island
The name is something of a misnomer. On a standard island-hopping tour, the deserted, picnic or uninhabited island

will be somewhere like Kuda Bandos, a rustic island affiliated to a resort, given over to day-tripping groups of tourists. Here you will probably have a barbecue followed by some snorkelling.

### Freestyle
The other option is to go it alone. Hire a speedboat and crew for the day and head off to the islands you fancy. The advantage is that your resort should help with any bureaucracy and you won't be travelling en masse. The downside is the cost, which can be upwards of $200–300.

### Resort island
This needs little by way of explanation. You will spend an hour or two in a different bar or on a different beach from usual.

### Village island
One stop is typically a village, or inhabited, island. Your escort will give you a brief tour of the village, which

may encompass the school, the mosque, the cemetery and some sites of local industry, like a boatyard. It will definitely encompass the local shopping area, where locals will use the Maldivian version of the hard sell – one friendly attempt to entice you into their shop and polite acceptance if you decline – to earn your custom.

What can be more interesting on village islands is to head off alone for a bit and wander the streets. You'll undoubtedly pass children playing, women preparing food and older people lazing around in swing seats. All usually respond positively to a request for a photo. But aside from these fortuitous and fleeting glimpses, the village island you're likely to see will not be representative of village life as it might be in the further-flung atolls where tourism has not yet established itself. The village islands on the resort trail are used for the overspill of the hotels themselves, and the air-conditioned apartments used by resort staff are in no way typical of Maldivian homes and conditions.

Villagers relaxing under a tree on a village island in North Male Atoll

# Wildlife

The Maldives' distinctive geography precludes the variety of land animals that can be found in neighbouring countries. Big game is wholly absent. There are no pigs (Islamic teaching deems them dirty), few cows (nowhere to graze), slightly more goats, and no dogs (another Islamic no-no). Unsurprisingly, the sea provides most of the country's rich wildlife. But aside from the fish (see pp104–5), there are several other creatures you may encounter on your trip. None of them represent much of a threat, and apart from mosquitoes and ants scurrying across your bathroom floor, most will be welcome sights.

A lizard spotted on Paradise Island

## Birds

Despite adverse conditions for most birds, around 150 species have been spotted in the Maldives, many of them migratory. One main kind is the heron, some of which are big and brave, quite at ease with camera-clutching tourists in their vicinity. Seabirds are naturally in the majority, with terns, frigate birds, noddies and tropic birds present. The main land birds are the house crow, which feeds on fish offal in the villages and is now so numerous it is regarded as a pest, and the koel, a cuckoo that uses the crow to host its eggs and which is heard (its call resembles a shriek) but not usually seen. Some dazzlingly coloured parrots can be spotted in and around Male; 150 live in the birdhouses constructed for them at Thulhaagiri (see pp52 & 149). Other avian visitors include hapless migrants who have been blown off course.

## Lizards

While dangerous reptiles are happily lacking (there are said to be very occasional appearances from crocodiles), one that you will most definitely encounter is the lizard. Colourful lizards are everywhere, outside your hotel rooms, climbing

A black-tip shark cruises near a water villa

trees and dashing across the pathway ahead of you. Afraid of people, they won't deliberately enter your room, but will often stay still long enough for a picture.

## Sharks

Sharks are one of the highlights for divers in the Maldives. There have been no reports of attacks (the apocryphal comparison is that you are more likely to be killed by a falling coconut). Rather it is the sharks that have most to fear from human contact, as they are still commonly hunted and their jaws sold as holiday souvenirs. According to the Ministry of Tourism, there are 37 different shark species in the country, a figure that is expected to increase. The ministry-led Shark Watch programme is intended to raise awareness about the creatures and liaise with tourists to improve sharks' contribution to the industry. The country was once famous for its shark feeding, but the practice has now largely ceased owing to fears it was too great an intrusion into the fish's natural routine and behaviour.

## Turtles

Long a source of food, sea turtles are now protected from trade by the Convention on International Trade in Endangered Species, and the Maldives has backed this up with its own laws. The loggerhead, leatherback, green sea turtle, Olive Ridley and hawksbill are all found in the country. They live largely at sea, with the female venturing onto land only to nest. She lays her eggs in the sand, the temperature of which determines their sex. After 60 days they emerge and head for the sea. Some resorts, including the Banyan Tree, are running conservation projects to boost population numbers (see pp70–71).

# Tour: Island cruises

*Apart from the half-day or full-day boat trips, the best way of seeing a lot of the Maldives without having to negotiate the bureaucracy is by overnight cruise. There are various ways of doing this, depending on your required levels of comfort and privacy and your budget. As well as the ground – or sea – you cover, another advantage of a holiday on the water is being able to see remote islands, far beyond the reach of the average package holidaymaker.*

## Safaris

The most basic cruise available is what the Maldivians call safari, with a *dhoni*-style boat that has been specially adapted to provide accommodation, with a motor, bathing facilities and sleeping cabins. To host tourists overnight, the boat must be registered with the Ministry of Tourism and have a safety certificate and permission to operate in this capacity. The website of the **Maldives Tourism Promotion Board** (*www.visitmaldives.com*) lists around 70 such vessels with contact details and each boat's specifications. Cabins may be totally separate with bunks, or just partitioned by curtains. Some boats have an element of mucking in, and you may be welcome (or required) to help out with the 'housework'. There is usually plenty of camaraderie among the passengers, which may not suit those who need their own space.

In line with the Maldivian government's frantic desire to keep locals and tourists apart, safari boats are restricted to the areas where tourism is already present, so it is unfortunately not possible to up anchor and sail off to the furthest reaches of the country. However, you will be able to see some of the more authentic and representative village islands, and uninhabited islands in the true sense of the word. There are also evening stops at resorts allowing passengers to have a few drinks in the bar. Meals may consist of fish caught by the crew, with some simple, non-perishable extras. Prices

The jetty at Banyan Tree Resort

vary depending on how much luxury you want, but the minimum is around $120 per person per day. Drinks (and sometimes food) may be extra.

## Diving safaris

One group to whom safaris are particularly suited is divers. While most safari vessels will offer some opportunity for diving, others will devote the whole trip to it, charting the route to take in some of the best sites the archipelago has to offer. Passengers, who are usually qualified and advanced divers, are accompanied on the trip by an experienced dive master and crew, and the equipment is brought along in a special *dhoni*. The route may change depending on the weather and the expected conditions at the dive sites. A typical itinerary includes two dives per day, some of which take place at night. In the evening the boat stops at a resort as on a standard safari.

## Cruises

For the safari experience with a touch more luxury (think sundecks and Jacuzzis), try a cruise. You might not be able to bring your own yacht, the option for high-net-worth individuals such as Roman Abramovich, but scheduled cruises are available for non-billionaires. The main name in the game is the *Atoll Explorer* (*see panel, p93*).

# One of the *Atoll Explorer*'s routes

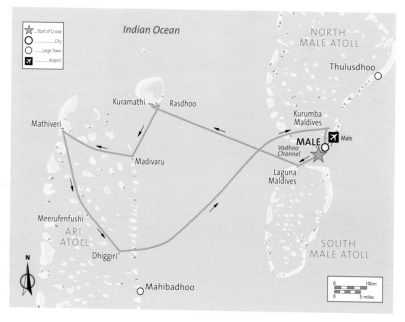

# Environmentalism

It is more than motivation to keep their islands and ocean pristine and pretty that gives the Maldivians a keen interest in environmentalism; the continued existence of the country itself is potentially at stake. With over 80 per cent of its islands less than 3½ft (1m) above sea level, the Maldives is in the front line in the battle against climate change and the accompanying rising sea levels, and its green efforts have taken place both at home and on the international stage.

It was the first country to sign up to the Kyoto Protocol, which sets targets for cuts in the greenhouse gas emitted by signatory nations, and the president subsequently wrote to

Turtles are not released into the wild during their first two years at Banyan Tree

George Bush – perhaps somewhat optimistically – to urge him to get the United States to follow suit. Meanwhile, back at home, the country is a keen participant in World Environment Day, with resort staff planting and cleaning, and educating local communities about the planet. Many resorts are taking measures individually to be more eco-friendly, hoping that the world does the same, and they have competed annually since 1999 for the President of the Maldives Green Resort Award. Winners include Banyan Tree, Soneva Fushi, Sun Island, Angsana and Coco Palm.

The government has also designated 25 diving sites as marine protected areas, where anchoring and most fishing are prohibited. It is encouraging forestation, to stop the sea eroding beaches, and the cleaning of the coral reefs, the islands' natural protection from tidal surges. School children are taught environmental science, which receives the same prominence in schools as writing and maths. There are also regulations in place to stop overdevelopment.

Banyan Tree, through the Green Imperative Fund – an optional contribution of $1 per guest per night which the company then matches – has several environmental projects in its Maldives resort, overseen by a full-time marine biologist and team. One involves guests, resort staff and local school children in coral transplanting. El Niño, the phenomenon that causes rises in ocean temperature, was responsible for accelerating coral bleaching in 1998, when an estimated disastrous 80 per cent of Maldives coral was destroyed (*see pp84–5*).

Another Banyan Tree project is trying to increase the numbers of turtles in the wild. Baby turtles' odds of survival are significantly less than 1 per cent. The resort has a nesting beach and releases the young into the wild at two years old, after which it monitors their progress through satellite tracking. Sharks are another beneficiary, and the resort is studying a small captive population to better understand their biology.

Other resorts are also doing their bit. At Royal Island, water is recycled and used for gardening, natural waste is burnt and the rest sent to Male for recycling, and no dirty water goes back into the sea. Biodegradable chemicals only are used in the laundry and the large machines run off gas, not electricity. Similar measures are in place on other islands. Many hotel rooms have notices proclaiming the huge amount of energy wasted by the global hospitality industry through washing clean towels, and they request that guests re-use them if possible.

# Ari Atoll

*After North Male Atoll in the early 1970s and South Male Atoll at the end of the decade, the next main wave of development came in the 1990s, when several islands in Ari Atoll were designated future resorts. One of the largest atolls in the country, at just under 80km × 30km (50 miles × 19 miles), it comprises Ari Atoll itself, along with Rasdhoo Atoll and the minuscule Thoddoo Atoll, famous for its watermelons and the archaeological finds of the 1950s that revealed its Buddhist history.*

Ari is sometimes known as Alifu, its alphabetical name (*see panel, p108*). It is approximately the same size as North and South Male Atolls combined, and lies to the west of them, slightly to the south. The atoll has around 10,000 inhabitants living on 18 islands. Because of the distance from Male, which can be as far as 96km (60 miles) for the southernmost islands, many resorts transfer guests by seaplane, which usually means you get a wonderful panoramic flight included in your holiday price. If you go by speedboat, the journey can take more than two hours. Travelling by *dhoni*, which would be very unusual, will take over double that.

Traditional livelihoods such as fishing, turtle hunting and coral gathering have gradually given way to tourism, with local people either working at resorts themselves or in auxiliary industries such as manufacturing souvenir handicrafts. To the chagrin of eco-campaigners,

however, shark hunting continues in earnest. Sharks are one of the big draws for divers, in particular the whale sharks that frequent some areas. The atoll does not generally have extensive tracts of barrier reef, but is rich in *thilas* (coral-covered structures protruding from the water) and dive sites.

## Angaga

Well-run Angaga was the first hotel to start operating in the new Ari Zone. Its beach, which goes right round the island, is superb even by the already phenomenal Maldivian standards. It's a small island bursting with palm trees and shade, its buildings' thatched roofs complement the natural aesthetic, and the restaurant design is inspired by the *dhoni*. The reef is nearby on one side, facilitating enjoyable diving and snorkelling, while the other side of the island looks out to the sandy lagoon, suited to windsurfing. The Angaga Thila is another good dive site. Overall, the resort has a laid-back, grown-up

0        10km
0        5 miles

Thoddoo

Veligandu

Kuramathi   Rasdhoo

Gangehi        Ukulhas

Mathiveri              Velidhu          Indian Ocean
Nika Island   Boduholhudhoo

Indian Ocean

Madoogali

Feridhoo        Maayafushi           Bathala

Gaathufushi
                              Halaveli
              Fesdu
Maalhos                              Ellaidhoo

Dhoni Mighili

Himandhoo

Moofushi      Athurugau

ARI ATOLL

Hagngnaameedhoo

Thudufushi                       Omadhoo
              Kuburudhoo
                              Mahibadhoo

Mandhoo

Angaga              Lily Beach
                                 Vilamendhoo
Conrad Maldives   Mirihi        Ranveli Village
Rangali Island        Maafushivaru
                  Machchafushi   Dhangethi

              Vakarufalhi   Kudarah

                        Dhigurah

Fenfushi              White Sands
Sun Island         Dhidhoo
Holiday Island   Maamigili

N

O .....Large Town

Conrad Maldives Rangali Island's underwater restaurant

atmosphere, with the evening programme arranged flexibly to suit the guests. The island lies in the centre-south of the atoll.

*Tel: 666 0510. Email: angaga@ dhivehinet.net.mv. www.angaga.com.mv*

## Conrad Maldives Rangali Island (formerly Hilton Maldives)

Although the global hotel brand seems rather inappropriate for a back-to-nature destination such as the Maldives, the Hilton has adapted its high-luxury concept to suit the local environs since it arrived in 1994. The rooms feature a lot of wood, coral and other traditional touches, as in many resorts, although some use Canadian red cedar and have very un-Maldivian features like flat-screen televisions. The resort's two islands, Rangali Finolhu and Rangali, are connected by a 500m (550yd) wooden bridge. The two are significantly different; one round, the other long and thin.

As you would expect with the Hilton name and prices, the hotel gives its guests the finest. There are two spas, in one of which you can observe the marine life through the glass floor during your massage. Similarly, you can dine in an underwater restaurant, said to be the only one in the world. There is also tennis, a fitness centre and a dive centre, although it is not a resort that attracts serious divers; few would want to pay Hilton prices then spend most of the day off the islands. The shallow lagoon renders snorkelling difficult, but it is possible near the reef. The site, on the western edge of the atoll, is also the westernmost resort in the country. *Tel: 668 0629. Email: Maldives@ hilton.com. www.hilton.com*

### Dhoni Mighili

A resort- and boat-based holiday in one, Dhoni Mighili houses its few guests in six luxury motorised *dhonis* (complete with air-conditioning and other mod cons), each of which comes with a crew and butler, as well as a thatched bungalow to which you can retreat when you want the ground to be stationary. The *dhonis* can sail off at your will, and can even make the journey from the east of the atoll, where the island is situated about one third of the way down, to the airport.

*Tel: 666 0751. Email: info@ dhonimighili.com. www.dhonimighili.com*

### Halaveli

One of the 'no news, no shoes' brigade, Halaveli prides itself on its laid-back, friendly ambience and is thick with palm trees. Its crescent shape is unusual, and it enjoys brochure-perfect beaches. The wide, shallow lagoon affords the usual gamut of water sports, swimming, snorkelling, catamaraning, windsurfing and parasailing, but it is diving that gets the most guests in. In 1990 the management sunk a 33m (108ft) freighter which forms part of an excellent reef. All of the rooms have been designed with coral and thatch.

A palm-fringed beach on Holiday Island

The on-island activities consist of evening entertainment, including cabaret on the resort stage, beach games, table tennis and darts. Halaveli is on the eastern side of the atoll, about a third of the way down.

*Tel: 666 0559. Email: halaveli@ dhivehinet.net.mv. www.halaveli.com*

## Holiday Island

Smaller than its sister and neighbour Sun Island, this verdant resort, the atoll's southernmost one, is nonetheless on the large side, at 700m × 140m ($3/8$ mile × $1/8$ mile). Whereas Sun goes for the families and younger crowd, much of Holiday Island's clientele is in the 30–45 age group, and it also sees a high number of honeymooners, attracted by the romantic touches such as candlelit dinners served right outside your room. It has lush, landscaped gardens and highly rated beaches. Nearby is Maamigili, an inhabited island that can be visited on the resort's island-hopping tour. All 142 rooms are in the same category and there are 9 adjoining family units. The island, whose previous name was Dhiffushi, has a jewellery shop run by a Sri Lankan company.

Despite its appeal to an older, peace- and quiet-seeking demographic, the hotel lays on entertainment, with a live band once a week and a culture show. There is beach volleyball and five-aside football for those who can bear the heat, as well as a gym, sauna, table tennis, tennis and snooker. A spa is

planned. The water sports and dive centres are at opposite ends of the island, and the former has waterskiing, windsurfing, jetskiing, parasailing, banana boat riding and canoeing. Because of the size of the lagoon, the reefs are relatively far; a boat takes snorkellers out to them about four times per day.

*Tel: 668 0022. Email: info@holiday-island.com.mv. www.villahotels.com*

## Kuramathi

A very rare exception from the 'one island, one resort' Maldivian rule, Kuramathi is home to three separate establishments, and guests are allowed to roam freely between **Kuramathi Village**, **Cottage**, and **Blue Lagoon**. Part of the reason this unusual set-up works is the size of the island; 1.6km (1 mile) long and up to 0.5km ($1/3$ mile) across. A minibus even shuttles guests between resorts.

Buddhist relics dating back over 1,000 years have been found on the island. Tourism arrived here early, in 1977. Ten years earlier the last of a declining population uprooted themselves to the nearby island of Rasdhoo, where resort guests can visit the school and mosque. The middle of the island is home to the Kuramathi Sports Club and a secluded section that is free of buildings. Almost every water sport one can think of is available here on the lagoon, and divers have a decent choice of sites, including Madivaru, or Hammerhead Point, a top-class site with great visibility, and a decompression chamber.

The three resorts have slightly different emphases. Kuramathi Village is a good-value resort frequented largely by young holidaymakers and independent travellers. The ambience is fun, and there's plenty of space. A slightly older crowd opts for Kuramathi Cottage, in the middle of the island, which has a more upmarket feel, while Kuramathi Blue Lagoon, the narrowest part of the isle, is so named due to its 20 over-water villas on the lagoon. The idea here is back to nature, with bougainvillea- and hibiscus-filled gardens and manta ray feeding at dusk. Kuramathi lies to the northeast of Ari Atoll.

*Tel: 666 0523/7/9. Email: cottage@ kuramathi.com.mv, village@kuramathi.com or blagoon@kuramathi.com. www.kuramathi.com*

Several resorts on Ari Atoll have spas

## Lily Beach

One of the latecomers to the area, Lily Beach is based on Huvahendhoo, a long thin strip of an island with sizeable beaches. The resort is run on an all-inclusive basis, which suits party-oriented holidaymakers expecting to have a high consumption, and the island has an active evening entertainment schedule of discos, live music, magic shows, *Bodu Beru* and beach games. There is also tennis and volleyball. Rooms have a modern feel and there are different categories of accommodation.

Some 50 sites are accessible through the dive centre **Ocean Pro** (*www.oceanpro-diveteam.com*), and other water sports on offer include windsurfing, canoeing, catamaraning and fishing. Only 10m (30ft) from the shoreline, the house reef also has a platform and is suited to beginners. On the eastern rim of the atoll, Lily Beach is about a quarter of the way from the southernmost end.

*Tel: 668 0013/4/5. Email: info@ lilybeach.maldives.com.*
*www.lilybeachmaldives.com*

## Nika Island Resort

Kudafolhudhu was an uninhabited island when it was leased in the early 1980s by Italian architect Giovanni Borgo, who built a bungalow in which to live out a tropical fantasy. With the addition of similar structures, the place metamorphosed into a hotel, but Borgo never lost sight of his original vision.

### A ROMAN MYSTERY

In 1958, Maldivian village labourers excavating a Buddhist *stupa* (mound) on Thoddoo Island, near to Ari, unearthed a beautiful coral casket containing a silver box, some rings and two coins. Cleaning the money revealed an animal on one side and a human head on the other. The coins were lost and then forgotten, until a visiting academic found a negative of one of them in the Maldivian archives. He sent a print to the UK, where British Museum staff identified it immediately as a Roman coin, minted in the first century BC. Of its journey from Rome to concealment at a Buddhist relic, little is likely to be discovered.

The villas are reached by a sandy track running between coral walls, in the style of a traditional Maldivian village. Each nestled in its own garden, the rooms were designed in the shape of a shell and decorated with local motifs like the *dhoni*. There are plenty of trees and plants – mango, papaya, watermelon, banana – which provide much of the fruit served to guests. In the middle of the island is a huge Banyan Tree, or *nika*, from which the resort takes its name.

The beaches at Nika make up for in beauty what they lack in size. Tennis and badminton are two of the ways to pass the time on land, and there's also an ayurveda massage centre for the less energetic. Water-based activities include windsurfing, canoeing, swimming and snorkelling, and there's a high-quality house reef. Divers can take PADI courses up to professional level, a walkway leads to a platform by the reef for nearby underwater action, and there are also good sites slightly further afield, such as Miyaruga Thila, particularly beloved of sub-aquatic photographers. And those who want to see the marine world without strapping oxygen onto their back or even getting wet can visit the large open-air aquarium. Nika is near the north of Ari.

*Tel: 666 0516. Email: nika_htl@ dhivehinet.net.mv*

### Sun Island Resort

Set on Nalaguraidhoo, at the southern tip of the atoll, Sun Island is one of the largest and most modern resorts in the archipelago. At 1.6km × 0.4km (1 mile × 1/4 mile), it has a perimeter of 4km (2½ miles), and is so big (in Maldivian terms, of course) that guests can hire bicycles to get around,

or take one of the golf buggies that operate as a free taxi service. It even accommodates an 18-hole golf course, finished in 2007. The beaches are wide and long, and the island is verdant. It is one of seven islands in its reef. Sixty-eight water bungalows and four presidential suites are accessible by a long jetty.

Sun Island has many of the latest high-tech features, such as in-room internet and bill-checking via your TV. This is a resort for the young, energetic and families. The number of bars reaches double figures, and the place lays on entertainment, such as stingray feeding, with a wide appeal.

There is also plenty to do in the ocean. Sun Island has two centres offering water sports: **Little Mermaid**, an external firm (*www.diveatsun-*

A tranquil Sun Island beach

*island.co.kr*); and **Gaastra**, Villa Hotels' own brand specialising in high-performance equipment for hardcore enthusiasts. There is varied diving in the vicinity, with boats leaving several times a day, and various PADI courses can be taken. The large lagoon lends itself to surfing, and catamaraning, windsurfing, waterskiing, canoeing, jetskiing, fun-tubing, wakeboarding, kneeboarding, snorkelling and parasailing are also on the menu.

Land-based options include tennis, basketball, squash, volleyball, badminton, table tennis, aerobics and a gym. The spa has 21 treatment rooms and offers hydrotherapy, aromatherapy massage, local traditional massage, a sauna, steam bath, chilled pool and Jacuzzi. Experienced staff can provide 100 different treatments, some of which draw on natural ingredients grown in the garden.
*Tel: 668 0088. Email: info@ sun-island.com.mv. www.sunislandmaldives.com*

## Thudufushi

This tiny island is the sister resort and neighbour of Athurugau in the centre of the atoll; the two are about 15km (9 miles) apart. Sometimes referred to as Thundufushi, it's an idyllic island with excellent beaches and copious palms. Its food gets rave reviews. The highly rated house reef makes the snorkelling here first class. For diving, Panettone, a wall brimming with crevices and caves, is close by, as is the rich Thudufushi Thila. The resort offers non-motorised water sports free of charge.
*Tel: 668 0597. Email: admin@ thudufushi.com.mv. www.planhotel.com*

## Velidhu

Sitting in the middle of some superior dive sites, Velidhu enjoys a good reputation among the diving community, not least for its environmental awareness. The large, sheltered lagoon allows for plenty of water sports, including waterskiing, catamaraning, snorkelling and banana

The view from a Sun Island water villa

boating. It's small enough for visitors to walk the perimeter on foot in ten minutes and it enjoys lush vegetation. After takeover by a Sri Lankan group, its facilities improved, although it is more about fun than luxury. Entertainment comes in the form of cultural shows, live music and a disco, and there is also an unusual Mongolian barbecue. Velidhu lies to the north and centre of the atoll. *Tel: 666 0551. Email: velidhu@ dhivehinet.net.mv. www.johnkeellshotels.com*

## Vilamendhoo Island Resort

Another of the larger islands that is strong on water sports and evening entertainment, Vilamendhoo is 0.9km ($^1/_2$ mile) long and up to 0.3km ($^1/_8$ mile) wide. Its diving is excellent – regarded by some as among the best the atoll has to offer – thanks in large part to the fact that many of the corals have avoided the bleaching effect suffered elsewhere, and that the local *thilas* are also attractive. Snorkellers can easily reach the house reef, which is similarly esteemed. The diving school runs a comprehensive service, with parasailing, waterskiing, catamaraning and windsurfing all possible, and the usual on-island recreation – gym, tennis, volleyball and snooker – can be found. A sandbank compensates for the small size of some of the beaches, and there are plenty of trees giving succour from the sun. Nights are often enlivened by a disco. Vilamendhoo is situated in the southern part of Ari Atoll.

*Tel: 644 4487. Email: sales-vilamendhoo@pch.com.mv. www.vilamendhoomaldives.com*

## White Sands

The popular Maldivian motto 'no news, no shoes' aptly sums up the relaxed ethos of White Sands, located at the south end of Ari Atoll. Regular evening entertainment make this one of the country's livelier islands. There is a mix of accommodation, with lower cost rooms as well as more expensive water bungalows built to resemble traditional Maldivian houseboats, which brings a more varied clientele. It has gone for the traditional materials of coral, wood and thatch in the construction, adding to the informal feel, and is a largely green island with a good range of beaches.

Despite the rather shallow lagoon, a variety of water sports is available, including kayaking, catamaraning, fishing, windsurfing, banana boating and fun tubes. Because of the distance, the resort takes snorkellers to the reef for free. The island's **Euro Divers** (*www.euro-divers.com*) centre has access to a variety of dive sites, with Kudarah Thila, Broken Rock and Dhigurah Thila all within about 10km (6 miles). On land, there is badminton, tennis, volleyball, board games and a book exchange. The Coconut Spa draws on time-honoured Asian massage practices and offers full body treatments. *Tel: 666 0513. Email: resort@ maldiveswhitesands.com. www.maldiveswhitesands.com*

# Tour: Scenic seaplane

*It is only from the air that you get a real impression of the country's extraordinary geography. Looking down on seemingly unending dark blue, dotted with distorted blobs of a lighter turquoise and within these, even smaller patches of golden sand, with white specks of boats making their way between, you will see the real Maldives in action. There are different ways of taking to the skies. The views will be largely the same, but the cost and the extras can vary.*

## 1 Airport transfer

The remote resorts (those in the northern and southern atolls), often whisk their guests between Hulhule and their hotel by seaplane, the price of which may already be included in the package holiday. Two companies, **Trans Maldivian Airlines** (*www.transmaldivian. com*) and **Maldivian Air Taxi Pte Ltd** (*mat@mat.com.mv*), provide the service, using small Twin-Otter aircraft that seat around 15 passengers. The flights are run professionally: passengers are met by resort or airport representatives who make sure you get in the correct airport bus and deliver you for your flight at the right time.

However, flights are subject to weather conditions and industrial action is not unheard of. If you do end up travelling during bad weather, the flight can be a little nerve-wracking.

## 2 Upgraded airport transfer

If your package does not include a seaplane flight to your hotel and your resort is very distant from Male, you can sometimes pay for an upgrade and go by plane instead of speedboat. Enquire at your resort desk at the airport or hotel reception.

## 3 Booking privately

As is typical of the Maldives, anything you might wish to do individually is problematic. The two airlines do not generally quote direct prices for resort flights to individual travellers. However, the companies want to fill empty seats, so it may be possible to negotiate directly, or get a seat as part of a locally arranged trip to a resort.

## 4 Scenic flight

Scenic flights can be booked either through your hotel or one of the airlines.

## 5 Charter

Anyone with a very comfortable budget can charter a seaplane. Expect to pay upwards of $2,000 an hour.

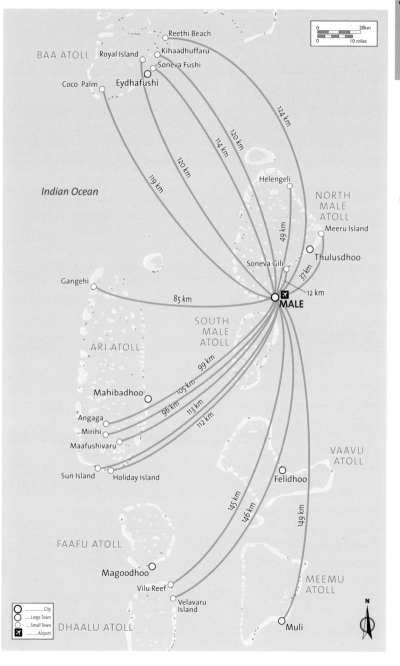

# Coral reefs

Coral reefs are ocean structures produced in shallow, warm water by living organisms. They are constructions of almost unfathomable complexity, with layers of dead polyps (cylindrical creatures related to the jellyfish) beneath a stratum of living ones. A reef consists of a colony of millions of polyps which, over generations, leave the limestone skeletons that make up the reef. Maldivian coral reefs also contain detritus and coralline algae, which acts as a kind of cement, binding the coral waste together. Few 'waste products' look so beautiful.

Corals start off as free-floating larvae, which soon become fixed to a hard surface to become polyps. A polyp can reproduce both asexually (dividing itself) and sexually (releasing egg and sperm into the sea, in a process known as coral spawning). Reefs grow upwards from the seabed, and need sunlight, so optimum development takes place 20m (65ft) or less below the surface of the sea. Corals can grow by as much as 25cm (10in) a year, or as little as a few millimetres. The Maldives is thought to have over 250 different types of coral, going down as far as 2,100m (6,890ft).

It is difficult to believe, with something that feels so hard and stony, but a coral reef contains as much life as a rainforest. When Maldivians tell you that the reef comes alive at night, they are referring to feeding time, when the polyps extend their tentacles to take hold of the plankton off which they feed. During the day, they retreat into their cylinders to avoid predators.

The Maldives is one of the few places to have coral reefs because the water here meets three criteria: it must be constantly warm, clear and shallow. When El Niño increased ocean temperatures in 1998, many coral reefs suffered significant bleaching, which is what happens when the coral colonies expel the algae (with which they usually cohabit in a symbiotic relationship, swapping nutrients for shelter). This turns the reef white, hence the term. The vast majority of Maldives coral was destroyed in 1998, although it has made a good recovery, thanks in part to the efforts of various resorts to protect and preserve it.

The coral reefs have long played a huge role in Maldivian life. For 300 years, before the arrival of concrete, coral was used as the building blocks

A coral reef at Banyan Tree

of houses, and today it is a major factor in luring divers to the islands. But its preservation does far more than just serve an industry. The reefs act as a barrier against the ocean, and without them, coastal erosion would devastate the low-lying islands. Many believe that the Maldives would have suffered far more severely from the 2004 tsunami had it not been for the reefs.

With both their livelihoods and lives dependent on the coral reefs, the Maldivians are experimenting with passing electric current through steel frames to try to coat the steel with limestone and attract corals, thereby stimulating reef growth. The pioneers of the technology believe that their artificially generated reef will sustain environmental challenges more robustly than the organic kind, and as a result help to stem the worldwide destruction of coral reefs.

# Northern Atolls

*The Northern Atolls are divided into seven areas, with the northernmost four in the country only now seeing their first incursion from tourism. From north to south they are Haa Alifu, Haa Dhaalu, Shaviyani and Noonu in one long, narrow chain, then Raa to the west of Noonu and Baa directly below it, with Lhaviyani to the east. The resorts here, being so far from Male, mostly have a calmer feel. In total, around 110,000 people live in the Northern Atolls.*

The northernmost islands, having had no tourism to sustain them until recent years, have relied on the Maldives' other main industry, with Haa Alifu in particular renowned for its fishing. It also contains some rare fertile land, which lends itself to agriculture, and bananas, papayas, and sweet potatoes are grown there. Less peaceably, British forces had a military base on the island of Kelaa during World War II, and its remains are still visible today. But now the region is looking towards the hospitality industry. Further resorts are set to join the pioneers who have set up shop in the past couple of years, as several more islands have been earmarked for resorts or have construction underway already.

Raa, Baa and Lhaviyani have been on the development trail for longer than their northern neighbours. They also have a significant fishing tradition. Alifushi, an island in Raa, is a centre of boatbuilding – certainly useful given the long journey to Male. Raa and Baa residents are also famed for their lacquerwork, while the Lhaviyani people are celebrated for their medicinal expertise plus their handicraft techniques using coral and mother-of-pearl.

All the northern islands see less traffic than the area round the capital, which means pristine waters for diving. The area's *kandus* (channels through the reef from the ocean to an atoll's lagoon) and many *thila* dives tend to attract advanced divers, owing to the strong currents.

### Coco Palm Resort

Coco Palm, based on Dhunikolhu Island, is the southernmost resort in Baa Atoll, some distance from the other resorts in the area which are bunched closer together towards the north. A clear horizon and few comings and goings make this a serene and exclusive destination. With less natural vegetation than some other islands, the management has done its best to

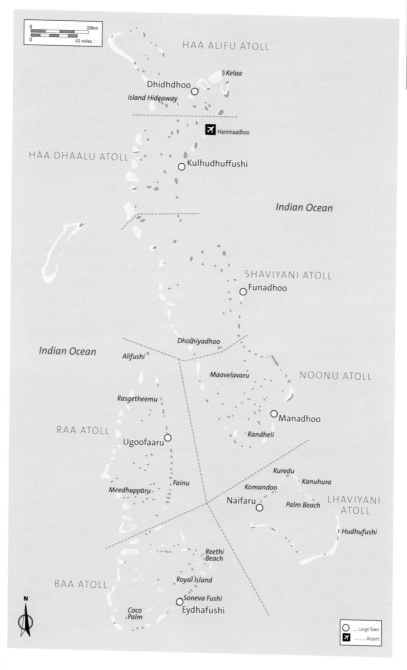

introduce more privacy- and shade-providing foliage. This is not a party place, rather a romantic one that would suit honeymooners, with champagne-fuelled moments for two and sunsets popular among guests. A spa overlooks the lagoon and there is also a gym and a tennis court.

The island boasts excellent beaches and good swimming. Beginners will enjoy snorkelling at the reef, which is fairly near to the shore, but although there is a dive centre this is not a big stop for the diving community or water-sports enthusiasts. Anyone who does try diving here, however, will find sites unspoiled by chains of visitors. The same applies to the local islands. *Tel: 660 0011. Email: cocopalm@ sunland.com.mv. www.cocopalm.maldives*

## Island Hideaway

One of the newest resorts, Island Hideaway on Dhonakulhi Island opened its doors in August 2005, and at the time of writing is the only resort in the entire Haa Alifu and Haa Dhaalu Atolls. At 1.4km × 0.5km ($^7/_8$ mile × $^1/_3$ mile), it is large, shaped like a half-moon, and thickly covered with coconut palms, banana trees and other foliage. Keen to pick up the yachting crowd, it has introduced the first marina in the Maldives. Further luxury can be found in the Mandara Spa. Prices reflect the upmarket ambience.

The house reef is 10–30m (30–100ft) away, and the resort boasts 20 untouched dive locations within an hour's journey. The diving school, **Meridis Dive** (*www.meridis.de*) offers free Nitrox to certified divers, among other services.

Snorkelling in the turquoise sea off Island Hideaway

An aerial view of peaceful Komandoo

*Tel: 650 1515. Email: sales@*
*island-hideaway.com.*
*www.island-hideaway.com*

## Komandoo

This haven of an island in the
northwest of Lhaviyani promises peace
and nature. Rooms are entirely of wood
and the other buildings have been
designed with a Maldivian aesthetic in
mind. But the island's forte is its
picturesque beaches. A nearby house
reef affords excellent snorkelling and
you may even spot dolphins among the
huge range of fish that frequent the
area. The shallow lagoon hosts free-of-
charge windsurfing and canoeing.
Numerous channels and *thilas* in the
area ensure a good choice of dive sites.
Operating since 1998, Komandoo is the
sister resort of Kuredu, and guests are

welcome to head over there if they want
to pass a livelier evening.
*Tel: 662 1010. Email: info@*
*komandoo.com. www.komandoo.com*

## Kuredu Resort

At the northern tip of Lhaviyani, for a
time Kuredu was the northernmost resort
until tourism surged past it. Outside the
main enclave of party resorts around
Male, this is one of the rowdier venues,
owing to the high number of guests
(there are 300 rooms), a choice of
drinking holes and many holidaymakers
opting for an all-inclusive deal, which
does not sit well with restraint. Partygoers
can recover from one too many in the
Maldivian Tea House, a pleasant venue
that adds a touch of local colour to
proceedings. At each end of the island is a
sandbar, to go with the decent beaches.

In daylight hours there is also plenty to do. A golf course opened in 2004 (one of the advantages of being based on a large island), and there is a wide range of water sports available. Free snorkelling lessons are given, and snorkellers can visit shipwrecks. The renowned diving centre is one of the largest in the country; PADI courses with multilingual instructors (reflecting the wide range of guest nationalities), a Nitrox station and underwater video cameras for hire are just a few of the facilities. Nearby is the Kuredu (Kuredhoo) Express, a drift dive and protected marine area. If you prefer to be above the water rather than below it, another option is to charter *The Britt*, a wooden sailing yacht with a crew of four that can be taken on day or night trips.

*Tel: 662 0337. Email: reservations@ kuredu.com. www.kuredu.com*

## Meedhupparu

The first, and as yet only, resort in Raa Atoll (although surely not for long) is a large island packed with amenities. As well as the usual recreational, health and pampering options – spa, sauna, Jacuzzi, steam bath, ayurvedic and herbal treatment pavilions – there's a shop where you can pick up gems and clothes, and even a hairdresser's. As you may expect from somewhere that offers so much to do, it's a vibrant, active resort which holds participation-led events like discos and theatre. There is also live music, although the entertainment is generally staged away

from the main bar so anyone who wants to sit it out can do so. A sizeable portion of the clientele is Italian, perhaps one reason for the island's sociable vibe.

In terms of natural highlights, the island is green, thick with palms and plants, and the beaches are large. With tourism still undeveloped in the atoll, the diving here has yet to be fully exploited and more sites will undoubtedly be discovered. At the moment the main points are Beriyan Faru Thila, a brilliantly coloured reef whose top is just 3m (10ft) below the surface, and Kottefaru Kuda Thila, a highly regarded site teeming with overhangs, caves and fish. Both are for advanced divers. Meedhupparu offers a range of other water-based pursuits in and around its shallow lagoon.

*Tel: 658 7700. Email: meedhupparu. com.mv. www.aitkenspenceholidays.com*

### IBN BATTUTA

Ibn Battuta was a 14th-century Islamic scholar, who made his name through his documentation of his travels over three decades. Journeys encompassing West Africa, the Indian subcontinent, South East Asia and China racked up more miles than Marco Polo, who slightly predated Battuta. He visited the Maldives twice, in 1343–4 and again two years later. It is his written account that forms the basis of the conception of the country's conversion to Islam, although it was the matrimonial laws rather than the history that seemed to impress him most: 'I had in the country four legal wives, besides concubines. I visited them all every day and spent the night with each in turn.'

## Reethi Beach

Set close to the northern rim of Baa Atoll, on the eastern side, Reethi Beach is not particularly close to any other resort island, which is often the case in the remoter areas, where tourism is only now picking up a pace. But it does have a number of uninhabited islands in the vicinity, to which it holds exclusive rights, affording ample opportunity for guests to take a break from the package resort atmosphere and go back to nature. The resort is keen to report that only 15 per cent of the island's surface area is covered by buildings, to ensure everyone gets his or her fair share of privacy and vegetation.

Authentic Maldivian architecture and green awareness are the two main design concepts at the resort, which started operations in 1998. It has a pretty beach that goes the whole way around the island.

It may be 'off the beaten track' – the journey to the island consists of a 35-minute seaplane flight followed by another 15 minutes in the hotel boat – but the place's relative remoteness does not mean it is dominated by the peace-and-quiet brigade; with five restaurants and two bars there is a social aspect to Reethi. It is also strong on activities. As well as the usual gamut of water sports, there is a wide range of land-based

*Northern Atolls*

A *dhoni* sails past Island Hideaway

things to do, from a sizeable gym and instructor-led aerobics sessions to darts and board games for the less energetically inclined. Villa-style accommodation comes in three categories, and there are duplex rooms for family groups or parties of friends. *Tel: 660 2626. Email: info@reethibeach. com.mv. www.reethibeach.com*

## Royal Island Resort

With sand so soft it feels like warm snow under the feet, dense foliage including seven Banyan trees, a mellow atmosphere and stylish rooms that blend a traditional wooden design with classy furniture and modern touches like in-room email access, it is easy to see why Royal Island's clientele includes such luminaries as Ricky Martin and Roman Abramovich. The island is all about relaxation. There is a pub where discos are organised, but they are usually cancelled because nobody shows up. Guests are more likely to head for the spa, designed in a Maldivian manner, and featuring a Jacuzzi, steam room and flower bath.

Horubadhoo, the island to the east side of Baa, on which the resort is situated, is long, and finding peace and privacy is easy. The preparations for the resort, which opened in 2001, unearthed some Buddhist relics, which were sent to the museum in Male. The island takes its eco-responsibilities

Beachside pools at Royal Island

seriously, recycling what it can and encouraging the staff to think green. There are two turtle breeding grounds on the island. Land sports are free, with the exception of tennis after 6pm, owing to the floodlight use. There is also a shop selling masks, drums and other traditional souvenirs.

The Dhigali Haa marine reserve, also known as the Horubadhoo Thila, is close to the island. It was designated a protected area because of its reef sharks and pelagics, which are a big draw for divers. The resort management has also recently installed a decompression chamber. With few tourists coming so far north, the dive sites are not as well traversed, and indeed more may well be found in the future. The lack of tourist traffic also makes the other excursions memorable. Foreigners traipsing through a village island is something relatively new to the people, unlike in places closer to the capital where boatloads have been pitching up every day for years, and the deserted islands really are deserted.
*Tel: 660 0088. Email: info@ royal-island.com. www.royal-island.com*

## Soneva Fushi Resort

You will probably reach Kunfunadhoo, the home of Soneva Fushi, by seaplane, where you dock at a tiny floating platform with a sign that reads 'Welcome to Soneva Fushi International Airport'. It is a humorously self-deprecating arrival to what is

considered by some to be among the best resorts in the country. Eco-friendliness is omnipresent here, from the bamboo that crops up everywhere to the natural materials – coconut, coral, stone, wood, clay and thatch – used in the design. The vegetation is similarly impressive, dense and diverse, affording lots of privacy, although with just 65 rooms on a 1.5km (7/8-mile) long island, that is never threatened. Guests all have access to a bicycle to cross the long distances.

Divers can take day trips to 30 different sites throughout the atoll, the snorkelling is very highly rated and there are all the usual water sports to choose from too. But many guests prefer to repair to the Six Senses spa for a massage overlooking the sea.
*Tel: 660 0304. Email: reservations-fushi@ sonevaresorts.com. www.sixsenses.com*

### ATOLL EXPLORER

If you don't want to be restricted to one island, or even one atoll, this converted oil-rig supply ship makes weekly tours around the country, based on two different itineraries. The 20 cabins come with air-conditioning and a private bathroom with hot water. Jacuzzis and sundecks provide a touch of luxury. There is an on-board PADI dive centre, themed evenings, a surprisingly varied menu with fresh vegetables and, of course, the opportunity to visit some remote areas and village and uninhabited islands largely untouched by tourism.
*Universal Enterprises Pvt Ltd, 39 Orchid Magu, Male. Tel: 332 2971. Email: explorer@ dhivehinet.net.mv*

# Diving

Aside from honeymooners and holiday-of-a-lifetimers, divers probably represent the main Maldives holiday market. The warm, clear waters, famous coral reefs and abundance of marine life attract novice and expert divers alike. The strictly controlled development of tourism has prevented the top dive sites from becoming spoiled by overuse, and the creeping spread of resorts to the furthest north and south Maldivian reaches has the promise of more sites awaiting discovery. Most of the best locations are in the channels between the open ocean and protected lagoon.

## Boat or island?

The first decision to make is whether to base yourself on a safari boat or an island resort. In general, conditions on shore are likely to be more comfortable – although some boats do have air-conditioned cabins, and larger ones even stretch to Jacuzzis – and possibly cheaper, but you will then be restricted to the dive sites in the area you've chosen. Thanks to the abundance of locations in the Maldives, this does not necessarily imply a small number. But serious divers, keen on reaching some of the more remote sites and prepared to risk cabin fever to do so, may prefer a live-aboard. This also has the advantage of a dive master who can plan the best stops based on the weather conditions and currents.

## Dive centres

If you opt for an island, it's worth researching its dive centre first. Almost all islands offer some diving, but the priority given to it and the attendant facilities (e.g. underwater camera or video camera, Nitrox, access to a nearby decompression chamber, etc.) may vary considerably. You should consider whether the sites in the vicinity are more suited to novices or advanced divers. Think, too, about whether you want to dive for purely recreational purposes, or whether you want to knuckle down to study and pursue qualifications.

## Timing

Timing is almost as important as location. The Maldives has two monsoon periods, which affect the weather, visibility and currents. The beginning and end of monsoon periods can be unpredictable, and it makes sense to take advice from a local expert.

Divers in scuba gear at Paradise Island

## Sites

Diving in the Maldives divides roughly into five categories. House reefs (where a resort beach runs straight onto the reef) suffer little from currents, a plus for beginners. *Giris* (underwater coral-covered structures that reach close to the surface of the sea) also offer fairly undemanding diving for learners, while *thilas* are similar to *giris* but peak lower, making them more challenging sites. Highlights are the coral growth, overhangs and varied reef fish. *Kandu* means 'channel' in Dhivehi, and this sees divers carried along past fish, caves and a range of absorbing pelagic activity. The shallow reefs and narrow channels so beloved of divers were a bane for vessels attempting to navigate the waters, many of which ended up on the ocean floor, providing the wreck dives that are the other main type of site.

## Children

Children mostly stick to snorkelling, but over-tens are legally allowed to dive. Some courses are available that teach children to scuba-dive in a resort swimming pool, a less scary beginning than going straight into the sea.

# Southern Atolls

*Below South Male Atoll, the infiltration of tourism has been slower than elsewhere. One reason is that the south of the country is more spread out than the north. Atolls here currently have one or two resorts at the most, although more have been allocated to developers. The most central, Vaavu, Meemu, Faafu and Dhaalu, form a rough square under South Male and Ari Atolls. Moving south, you come to Thaa, Laamu, Gaafu Alifu and Gaafu Dhaalu, then Gnaviyani and Seenu. In total they are home to nearly 120,000 Maldivians.*

Many safari boats navigate Vaavu, the northernmost of the upper bunch of atolls, which is still relatively undeveloped in spite of its proximity to the capital. Felidhoo and Fulidhoo islands are well known for their traditional dances. Beneath Vaavu is Meemu, where fishing and agriculture back up the fledgling tourism industry. With little doing in the way of farming or fishing, the main claim to fame of Dhaalu, west of Meemu, is its gold- and silversmiths. Completing the set is Faafu, previously a centre of Hinduism. Seven temples were discovered here. Aptly for the Maldives, their stones were used to build the country's second oldest mosque in the 12th century.

Thaa is fertile fishing territory, with various islands known for mat-weaving and carpentry. Laamu has some of the country's best-preserved ruins, some of which suggest a significant Buddhist heritage. Gaafu Alifu and Gaafu Dhaalu also have their fair share of ancient sites. Across the equator is Gnaviyani, an atoll and island in one, noteworthy for its two freshwater lakes and rich agricultural output.

But perhaps the most distinctive is Seenu, the southernmost atoll. The UK based troops on Gan during World War II, and a decade later installed a Royal Air Force base. Subsequently they linked the four main islands with a road, making it possible to walk, ride or drive for 17km (11 miles) in the same direction without hitting the sea – extraordinary in the Maldives. Visitors do not need a permit to visit the atoll, making it one of the most appealing to independent travellers and the easiest place, outside Male, to see authentic Maldivian society.

### Alimatha Aquatic Resort

The full title of this resort in Vaavu Atoll, Dhiggiri's sister island, indicates its emphasis. This is another diver's island, as scuba enthusiasts seek out

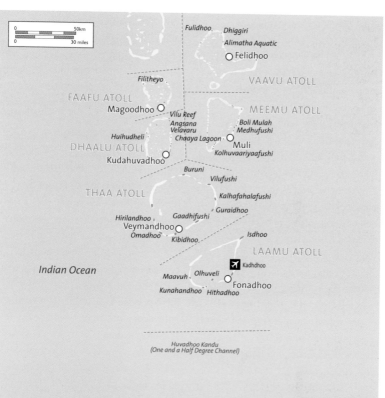

virgin diving territory. It has an impressive range of diving-related facilities, such as a decompression chamber, which are still relatively rare throughout the country, and an underwater photography school. The lagoon is shallow, and other water sports are also in demand here, with windsurfing and sailing popular among them. The island itself has a good, uninterrupted beach, and is thick with shady palms. Despite several changes in focus since it started up in 1975, Alimatha has a quintessentially Maldivian aesthetic about it. Both boats and seaplanes make the airport transfer; the former's journey across the Felidhoo channel can be choppy and anyone with a sensitive stomach might prefer to book the seaplane.

*Tel: 670 0575. Email: alimatha@ dhivehinet.net.mv. www.alimatharesort.com*

### Angsana Velavaru

One of the newest resorts to have opened its doors in the Maldives, the island is now under the management of Angsana, part of the Banyan Tree group, and joins a charming sister resort, Ihuru (in the middle of North Male Atoll). This branch, however, is in the far less crowded Dhaalu, currently home to only one other resort. Still waiting for tourism to start its inevitable colonisation of the area, it is relatively unspoiled (although as usual the concepts of 'spoiled' and 'unspoiled' must be interpreted in the Maldivian

way). The absence – for the time being, at least, although the situation must surely be temporary – of a plethora of competing resorts means that the nearby dive sites are pristine, and more will possibly be discovered as tourism makes headway. The nearby deserted islands are similarly away from the tourist trail.

The site's original name is Velavaru, which translates as Turtle Island, and the appellation is derived from the former residents who made their homes on the large beaches. The hotel operators have seized upon the connection, and the accommodation has been designed with something of a turtle theme (of course with the usual low-key good taste of the Banyan Tree), with semi-circular, turtle-shaped rooms of a unique design. Some come with luxurious extras such as a jet pool, and there are two very opulent presidential suites, in the form of the Angsana Villa (actually a combination of four different villas) and the only slightly smaller Velavaru Villa. In total, the resort has about double the capacity of its sister resort on Ihuru, with 84 rooms, most of which look out over the sea. All the communal buildings have been fashioned out of timber and thatch, with sand-covered floors preserving the authentic and relaxed aesthetic. In common with the Angsana ethos, the resort has a funkier design vibe than the average resort, and the natural materials are enlivened with dashes of bright colour and contemporary touches.

For dining, guests have the option of the buffet meals that come as part of the all-inclusive package, or paying extra to eat in the à la carte restaurant. The main gastronomic themes are Asian and Mediterranean. There is also excellent shopping in the gallery, a trendy boutique that's in another retail world from the often lacklustre resort shops elsewhere. Fairly little of it may have originated in the Maldives, but there is a great range of gifts and mementos for anyone into their candles, incense and essential oils. Divers have some 30 sites within an hour's journey, and the house reef is a ten-minute boat journey away. The spa is another plus point.

*Tel: 676 0028. Email: reservations-maldives@velavaru.com. www.velavaru.com*

### Chaaya Lagoon Hakura Huraa

The first resort to be opened on Meemu Atoll, Chaaya Lagoon Hakura Huraa is situated on the east side, slightly over halfway down. Its unusual configuration sees the majority of accommodation (70 out of 80 rooms) in the form of water bungalows, as reflected in the name Hakura Huraa, meaning 'reef above water'. The island is set in one of the longest stretches of reef in the country, with the house reef about 1km (²/₃ mile) away. Water sports are available dependent to some extent on high tide and there is a wreck nearby for divers. Guests have access to a neighbouring deserted island. Recently refurbished, the resort has two restaurants and a lounge bar.

*Tel: 672 0014. Email: htlres.khms@ keells.com. www.chaayahotels.com*

Southern Atolls

The water villas at Chaaya Lagoon Hakura Huraa

## Dhiggiri

Remote and rustic, the small island of Dhiggiri caters mostly to water-sports enthusiasts. Its house reef is nearby and pretty, and the lagoon is similarly attractive. There is little in the way of organised entertainment. Operational since 1982, this is Maldivian hospitality the traditional way, where plasma is a biological term rather than a technical one.

Tel: 670 0593. Email: dhiggiri@ dhivehinet.net.mv. www.dhiggiriresort.com

## Filitheyo

One of the biggest islands, and also considered one of the most beautiful, Filitheyo opened in Faafu Atoll in 2002. It is entirely sheltered by a thick forest of palm trees, which maintain a high level of privacy. Both its beaches and its shallow lagoon are well regarded, with the latter having proximity to the beach and a large drop-off in its favour. The downside is that much of the coral is dead. The thatched roofs and extensive use of wood in the construction preserve a simple authenticity. With little competition in its atoll – it was the first resort to open here – the local dive sites remain in pristine condition, and this has led to the establishment of Filitheyo as a diver's resort. Partly owing to their early mornings, there is not much in the way of late-night happenings.

Tel: 331 6131. Email: fili@aaa.com.mv. www.aaa-resortsmaldives.com

## Gan

Over half a century of British presence has left its mark on Gan, most obviously with an airport and a road – not the prettiest of accoutrements, but certainly practical, and with the unintended effect of opening up an area for boat-free sight-seeing and exploration. The road links Gan to Feydhoo, Maradhoo and the capital Hithadhoo, all of which have interesting stops such as mosques, cemeteries and parks worth a look, and Hithadhoo even has a lake that's rich with avian life.

The first resort to set up here was **Equator Village**, a budget (again, that's in Maldivian terms) hotel that occupies the former sergeants' mess of the British era. Bicycles can be hired if you want to see more of the area. Divers come here for the large fish, the coral, which escaped much of the bleaching that occurred elsewhere, and the wreck of *The British Loyalty*, an oil tanker torpedoed by a Japanese submarine (*see panel below*).

### THE BRITISH LOYALTY

Doing her bit for the UK's war effort, in 1940 motor tanker *The British Loyalty* survived five assaults from a German aircraft off Scotland almost unscathed. But she was not so lucky in 1942 near Madagascar when she was torpedoed by a Japanese submarine and evacuated, with the loss of six lives. But the ship was believed to be salvable, and she was raised at the end of that year and either towed or sailed under her own power to Addu Atoll in the Maldives, to be used as a fuel storage hulk. She was located and again torpedoed by the Germans, this time irretrievably, and is now popular with scuba-divers.

The Sunset Bar and pool at Filitheyo

*Tel: 689 8721. Email: equator@*
*dhivehinet.net.mv.*
*www.equatorvillage.com*

### Medhufushi

This serene island in Meemu has a natural ambience, with thatched roofs, ample palm trees – some of which overhang the beach in that way that photographers love – and superb long beaches. The island, which is long and thin, started operating as a resort in 2002. It has a large, sandy lagoon which lends itself to the usual range of water sports, and while the reef is at quite a distance, the hotel sends out boats for snorkellers daily. This is a quiet getaway for the laid-back.
*Tel: 672 0026. Email: medhu@*
*aaa.com.mv. www.aaa.com.mv*

### Vilu Reef Resort

Vilu Reef Resort is on Meedhufushi in Dhaalu, not to be confused with Medhufushi in Meemu. It's a small, pretty island, held by some to be the best-looking of the post-2000 wave of resorts. There's plenty of shade from the palm trees and other well-developed vegetation. Like many of the resorts in this part of the country, the main emphasis is on diving, owing, in the main, to the proximity of so many temptingly unspoiled sites. Water sports, too, are popular. The relatively nearby house reef has a sheer drop-off which ensures excellent snorkelling; dolphins and sharks sometimes cruise by. Currents in this area can be strong, however. As in other predominantly diving-oriented resorts, there is not much action of an evening, although there are karaoke facilities. A spa, gym and billiards are the other on-land options.
*Tel: 676 0011. Email: info@*
*vilureef.com.mv. www.vilureef.com*

# Tour: Gan and Seenu Atoll

*Gan and its atoll are the one chance in the Maldives to set off on land and travel in the same direction without reaching the sea in a few minutes. If you don't fancy hiring a bike, the same route can be done by taxi, and the Equator Village resort does a similar tour by minibus.*

*Allow at least half a day. The route is 11 miles each way.*

*Start at the British War Memorial Garden just off the main road that runs through Gan, directly opposite the Seenu Gan branch of the Bank of Maldives.*

## 1 British War Memorial Garden

This pleasant, neat garden is so British in design that, were it not for the hot weather and dried-out grass, it could quite easily be in the UK. The memorial lists the regiments whose men fell in the service of their country. Two cannons close by, which have been there since 1972, were active in the defence of the atoll during World War II.

*From here, take the bridge over to Feydhoo, a residential island. Bear to the left and take the first main road running northwest into the island (continuing in the same direction in which you set off). After about 400m (¹/₄ mile) you will come to the school.*

## 2 Feydhoo School

The school is a large building and if it's a school day the hubbub from inside is cheering. Passing along the road itself gives an insight into authentic local life. There's also an old tomb next to the school.

*Continue along the road until you come to the sea. Bear right and cross the bridge into Maradhoo. Follow the coastal road round to the right for 1.5km (2 miles) until you see the school. Behind it is the cemetery and mosque.*

## 3 Mosque and cemetery

The British evacuation of the inhabitants from Gan in 1956 led to the establishment of two Friday mosques on Maradhoo. This mosque is the island's oldest and the cemetery its largest.

If you need a rest at this point – the next cluster of sights is 10km (6¹/₄ miles) away – there is a park a short walk up the road which looks out over the port.

*Carry on until the very end of the road. You'll pass the stadium, which is worth a stop if there's a match on. The road* bears sharply left. After about 400m (¹/₄ mile) you'll come to the centre of Hithadhoo, the capital.

## 4 Hithadhoo centre

The centre has a modern mosque, built by a local entrepreneur, and a school, whose cadets sometimes practise on the beach. There are tea houses around if you want a break.

*Turn right after the school and continue until the road ends. In front of you will be the lake, Eedhigali Kilhi.*

## 5 Eidhigali Kilhi

This fresh-water lake is one of the country's most highly rated bird-watching sites.

*Carry on north to the Koattey beach area.*

## 6 Koattey

This very densely vegetated part of the island has been declared a protected area. It's a picturesque place and there are some remains of a fort, built by a Sultan 250 years ago, which was demolished in the late sixties.

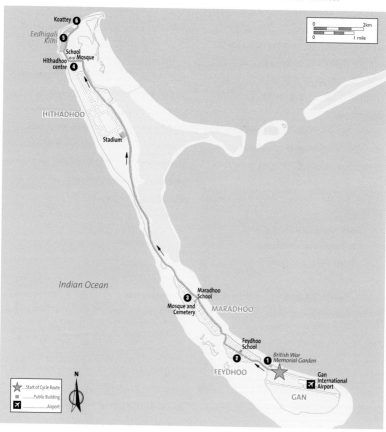

# Fish

One of the most popular holiday souvenirs in the Maldives (although admittedly there is not much choice, owing to the country's limited manufacturing base) is a set of three posters entitled 'Common Fishes of Maldives'. The wall charts are bright affairs, with all sorts of improbably weird and wonderful looking things illustrated and labelled. The diversity of the species swimming around just off the islands is quite overwhelming, from minnows of a few centimetres in length to whale sharks of 10m (33ft) and above.

You do not have to be willing to strap oxygen to your back and submerge yourself to have access to the country's diverse marine world. Even just walking along the jetty at your resort, a plethora of sea creatures will be visible just below the surface, the unpolluted waters ensuring excellent visibility. Aquarium-style facilities can also be found at some resorts, from Nika's open-air aquarium to the underwater spa at Huvafenfushi (*see p151*) and the Hilton's subaquatic restaurant (*see p74*).

If you're prepared to go to a bit more effort than lying on a massage bed to see some fish, snorkelling is a fairly easy way to begin, once the mask and breathing apparatus are mastered. Even children and weak swimmers will be able to manage, particularly as house reefs, with their abundance of fish, are often close to the beach or linked by a jetty or platform. Serious fish fans will want to go the whole way and scuba-dive, and waterproof versions of the Maldivian fish posters can be bought so that you can take them underwater with you and try to identify what you're swimming with.

There are obvious difficulties in quantifying Maldivian fish exactly, but estimates range between 700 and 3,000 species, making the country one of the most diverse marine

Shoals of fish are easily spotted in the clear waters

The islands are a paradise for snorkellers

environments in the world. Lagoons in the country are home to legions of fish attracted to coral, including the blackfooted clownfish (*Amphiprion nigripes*), unique to the area, and young, whitetip reef sharks (*Triaenodon obesus*), small creatures whose size and demeanour make them a handy 'gateway' for the timid to the world of larger sharks. Even within the lagoon the vividness and diversity are exhilarating, and the ocean brings even greater treasures, such as the unicornfish (*Eumecichthys fiski*) who shares a spiky horn with its legendary namesake. Other bizarre-looking creatures named after non-marine objects include the guitar shark (*Rhina ancylostoma*), the cowfish (*Lactophrys quadricornis*), which has two horns, although the dazzling oranges, greens and yellows in which they come are decidedly

non-bovine, and parrotfish from the family Scaridae, whose radiant colouring is more than a match for its avian equivalent's plumage.

Some of the weirder species even cause a rumpus among Maldivians. A rarely spotted ocean sunfish (*Mola Mola*) that washed up on Maradhoo island in Addu atoll was at the centre of a media storm in July 2007. The creature has the aspect of a fishhead minus a tail, with its main body flattened laterally, and older Maldivians call it the Dhivehi phrase for 'half a fish'. After a great deal of interest was generated on the island (and in the national papers), and as the ill-starred creature gradually expired, it was eventually identified by a Male diving school, before its burial was overseen by the police and the Maldives National Defence Force.

# Getting away from it all

*It is hard to define the concept of 'getting away from it all' in the Maldives, when coming to this idyllic archipelago and kicking back on a stunning tropical island is in itself an escape from the pressure and irritations of everyday life. Peace and quiet, privacy, stunning views, hot sun – all are practically guaranteed regardless of what island you go to. What is there to want to get away from?*

That said, the costs and infrastructure of travel in the country does persuade some people who normally travel independently to go for a package deal, the atmosphere of which might not suit them. Even regular package holidaymakers can get fed up with seeing the same faces for two weeks, particularly on the smaller islands. Even in paradise a change can be welcome.

First you need to decide what exactly you want to get away from. If you're a natural urbanite, and all the quiet, calm and neighbourliness of the staff and

Sailing towards an uninhabited island

guests' constant 'good evenings' is starting to grate, getting away from it all could be a trip to Male, whose noise, traffic and general bustle will be the ideal antidote to island fever. But if you're after a different kind of escape, there are several options, most of which are possible from wherever you are based.

## Chartered boat

A good way of escaping the crowds is by boat, the preferred method of celebrities (Roman Abramovich, Tom Cruise and Katie Holmes, and Beyoncé and Jay-Z have all chartered yachts for their Maldives trips). The accommodation in Dhoni Mighili, in Ari Atoll, consists of six *dhoni*-style motorised boats (with their own day bungalows), which can be decoupled and sailed around at will. Kuredu, in Lhaviyani, also has a yacht, *The Britt*, which can take up to ten people out by day or night. Most resorts have speedboats that with prior notice can be put at the disposal of guests for the day. The crew will take the vessel wherever you wish (depending on weather conditions and where they are legally permitted to go). Or you can charter a boat for the entirety of your stay and head off to a remote part of the country.

## Uninhabited islands

The concept of desert islands conjures up images of Robinson Crusoe, alone (apart from Friday) with nothing but a palm tree on his small scrap of sand in the middle of the sea. But 'uninhabited' does not always reflect that in the Maldives. Technically, resort islands are categorised as uninhabited, as are the small isles attached to them where they send boatloads of day-trippers. The result is that the uninhabited islands can seem busier than anywhere else. But on some occasions, uninhabited or deserted means just that. Some resorts, such as Fesdu, have tiny islands or sandbanks where guests can spend the day alone, having a picnic and lazing in the sun. As a wonderfully old-fashioned safety precaution, Fesdu staff give the voluntarily marooned couple a flag to hoist in an emergency. Champagne breakfasts or sunset dinners for two are other ways of escaping your fellow guests.

Others go one step further. Coco Palm gives its customers the chance to enjoy a barbecue dinner on a nearby island, then stay there overnight totally alone, with a walkie talkie in case of an emergency.

Of course, if your budget is flexible, there is always the option of renting an island yourself. Dhoni Mighili can be rented for up to 20 guests for $12,000–20,000 (£5,950–9,915) a night, all-inclusive. Reethi Rah is even more expensive. The island itself and the services of its 600 workers can be yours for $1 million (£495,000) for five nights. If your wallet will not quite stretch to a whole island, you could just go for a part of one. Soneva Gili's The

Private Reserve consists of two master suites plus guest accommodation in a separate section, accessible only by boat. It has its own private spa, gym and kitchen, plus two butlers available 24 hours a day. The price is not advertised.

## Village islands

The other aspect of a Maldivian holiday that you may need a break from is the hospitality. It is not that it is unwelcome, but the constant politeness and deference of the staff and the obligatory exchange of greetings whenever you pass another person can become wearing. Additionally, as many of the hotel chains are international, they serve up the national cuisine of the majority of their guests, and at the end of the trip everything is paid for in US dollars. Sometimes it feels that nothing you're experiencing – apart from the beach and the sea – is truly Maldivian. To get away from any such artificiality, the best option is a village island. Ostensibly, there is plenty of choice – 200 of them. However, many of the remoter ones are difficult to reach because of the bureaucracy and difficulty of finding an islander to sponsor your visit. The more central ones, particularly in the busy North Male Atoll, are now so used to foreign tourists that they are more like adjuncts to resorts than true villages.

A happy medium is to find a village island that has close connections with a resort, in order to circumvent the bureaucracy, but in an atoll that has not been significantly commercialised, and where the advent of tourists is relatively novel, so that there is still a level of authentic life.

Another choice is Seenu Atoll, the southernmost part of the country (*see pp102–3*). It is the only place in the whole country (excluding Male) where a hotel is situated in an area that is also a normal village. The road that connects Gan to its adjoining islands allows you to see local life without a boat or a permit.

### ATOLL NAMES

With the original atoll names deemed too elongated for foreigners to grasp, a system was devised to assign each a letter of the Dhivehi alphabet. These are now commonly in use, although you may sometimes hear the traditional names being used. The list below should help avoid confusion.

| | | |
|---|---|---|
| A | Haa Alifu | North Thiladhunmathi |
| B | Haa Dhaal | South Thiladhunmathi |
| C | Shaviyani | North Milahunmadulu |
| D | Noonu | South Miladhunmadulu |
| E | Raa | North Maalhosmadulu |
| F | Baa | South Maalhosmadulu |
| G | Lhaviyani | Faadhippolhu |
| H | Kaafu | Male |
| I | Alifu | Ari |
| J | Vaavu | Felidhu |
| K | Meemu | Mulakatholu |
| L | Faafu | North Nilandhe |
| M | Dhaalu | South Nilandhe |
| N | Thaa | Kolhumadulu |
| O | Laamu | Hadhdhunmathi |
| P | Gaafu Alifu | North Huvadhu |
| Q | Gaafu Dhaalu | South Huvadhu |
| R | Gnaviyani | Fuvahmulah |
| S | Seenu | Addu |

A village shop in Villingili

# When to go

*The Maldives is a year-round destination, and its tourist industry is not brought to a halt by its monsoons to the same extent as other Indian Ocean destinations such as Goa, for example. You can plan your trip in the most monsoon-hit month and still see a respectable amount of sunshine. The driest months correspond roughly with the European winter. Whenever you choose to go, you will only ever feel cold if you're standing near a particularly intense air-conditioning unit.*

The weather's worst manifestations are wind, rain and storms. Temperatures range from about 23°C (73°F) at night to 33°C (91°F) during the day, with little variation throughout the year, and the sea breeze provides respite from the sometimes oppressive heat.

That said, if you want to be sure of picture-perfect cloudless skies, the time to travel is between December and March, which coincides with *iruvai* (the dry northeast monsoon). This is peak season in the Maldives, with occupancy rates around 100 per cent, and you should aim to book well in advance. Prices are high in this period, with daily room rates as much as two to three times the figure demanded during the rest of the year. This is only partly due to the climate in the Maldives; the destination is still largely dependent on the European market, and demand rises during winter, dropping off somewhat when Europeans can find hot beaches closer to home.

April to October sees the advent of *hulhangu* (the southwest monsoon), which brings with it storms, wind, rain and clouds. June is usually the wettest month. Because of its tropical climate, the weather is unpredictable and subject to sudden changes. You can be having lunch, wondering how to spend the sunny afternoon ahead, only to find that by the time you've finished eating the balminess has turned to torrential rain. The advantage of this is that bad weather seldom lasts for too long.

Your choice of when to go, therefore, is likely to be influenced by your budget, plus the importance you attach to guaranteed good weather and solitude. While some resorts, particularly the more exclusive ones with the fewest rooms, see trade dip little in low season, occupancy at the larger ones can fall by as much as half, so a visit then can ensure you more privacy and space on the beach – not that this is lacking in the island nation whenever you go. The reduced rates also put the Maldives within reach of lower-budget travellers in this period. August is something of an anomaly, when demand is up again as a result of European holiday time.

One group who may need to pay more attention to the monsoon seasons is divers. The changing conditions affect currents, visibility and the chances of spotting certain fish. Divers also need to keep the season in mind when they choose their accommodation, if they wish to be best placed to reach the most well-favoured dive sites during that period; the best dive site in June may not be the best one in October.

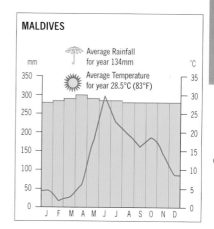

**MALDIVES**

Average Rainfall for year 134mm

Average Temperature for year 28.5°C (83°F)

### WEATHER CONVERSION CHART

25.4mm = 1 inch
°F = 1.8 × °C + 32

When to go

The warmth lingers until sunset in the Maldives

# Getting around

*Getting around in the Maldives is either very straightforward or a huge challenge depending on what you want to do. If you're staying on your resort island, it is simple: you walk. Even the largest islands are little more than a mile or so wide, and almost everything you wish to reach – beach, restaurant, spa, diving centre, shop – will be a few minutes' walk away. To explore other islands with any degree of independence is quite another matter, and will require high amounts of organisation and usually money. The cheap boats used by locals are typically closed to foreign tourists.*

However you travel, conditions will generally be good. Some boat trips are more luxurious than others, with leather seats, cold towels and complimentary drinks, but tourists seldom face discomfort. Seaplane travel may be difficult for anyone with restricted mobility, but both tourist and local boats (to a lesser extent) can largely be used fairly easily by travellers with disabilities, with the helpful crew willing to make any necessary arrangements.

## Boats

Given that 99 per cent of Maldivian territory is sea, if you want to travel around a bit, boats will figure prominently. Almost all resorts organise some trips off the island, to other, close-by resorts, village islands and Male, if they are near enough to the capital. But outings of a more independent nature are trickier, not to mention costly. And there are various barriers in place to deter you. In an attempt to preserve the Maldivians' Islamic lifestyle, the government is keen to prevent the free mingling of tourists and locals, and permission from the Ministry of Atolls Administration in Male is needed to visit inhabited islands. Even if you wish to visit other resort islands, things are not straightforward. Many are booked solid, so turning up on a whim and hoping to stay the night is unadvisable, even if you can find a boat to take you. Some will charge your boat a docking fee, even if you only want a meal in the restaurant. Further bureaucracy comes in the form of an $8 (£4) bed tax per tourist per night, which only authorised people are allowed to collect. The companies that run the resorts protect their security by keeping a close eye on comings and goings, so hopes of unfettered island exploring are unrealistic. The Maldives is not a place geared up for the independent traveller.

*Dhonis* are fairly slow but they are relatively cheap to hire

There is also the issue of the boat itself. For optimum freedom and choice, the best option is to hire a speedboat. This can be done either in Male or through your resort. Expect to pay upwards of $200, perhaps even two or three times that. You can also charter a cheaper but slower *dhoni*, the local boat originally designed as a fishing vessel which is distinctive for its curved bow, now largely motorised. This is still likely to cost around $100 for the day. Vessels for hire can be found along the waterfront in Male near the presidential jetty.

Another option is to try to use the resort-owned boats which travel to and from the airport island, picking up and dropping off passengers. However, these do not work to a regular timetable, but are scheduled around flight arrivals and departures, which can entail a lot of waiting around in the event that a flight lands a few hours late. Even when they are not full with airport passengers the crew will probably not be allowed to take you unless you have pre-arranged your visit. If you do decide to try this approach, go to the relevant resort's airport desk.

If you're determined to see something more of the Maldives than the usual resort-Male-day trip combo, perhaps the best way is to consult a local travel agent, who may be able to navigate the various bureaucracy and hurdles on your behalf.

### Cars and taxis

Due to the country's unique geography, the transport situation in the Maldives is unlike that in most other destinations. There is no line of car hire outlets at Male International Airport. Indeed, you are very unlikely to see the inside of a car throughout your trip. Taxis operate in Male and Gan, but it's normally the desire to escape from the heat rather than the need to cover any significant distance that persuades both tourists and locals to take them. They cannot usually be flagged down, but must be booked by phone. Local shopkeepers and hotel staff will often oblige. Private cars in Male tend to be used as a status symbol rather than a practical necessity, with the usual modes of petrol-powered transport being motorbikes and delivery vans.

### Ferries

A more serene way to get around Male and its surrounding islands is by ferry. Foreigners can take the frequent ferry from Male to the airport island of Hulhule, and the one from Male to Villingili. Not only is this a cheap and efficient way to get around (a one-way ticket to Villingili, on sale from a small office at the departure point, is just Rf3), it is also a pleasant way to see a bit more of local Maldivian life. Inter-island ferries are for locals only.

### Motorbikes and bicycles

In Male, bikes are popular – and practical given Male's warren of tiny streets – and both bicycles and motorbikes can be rented in the capital. While Male's traffic chaos is mild compared with nearby capitals such as Colombo and Delhi, it may come as something of a shock to newcomers to the region. Drivers and riders display a rather cavalier attitude to pedestrian safety, and with few useful pavements you need to keep your wits about you when walking around. Only experienced and confident cyclists and motorcyclists should consider hiring a bike.

### Seaplane

Undoubtedly the most exciting way to get around the atolls and islands is by seaplane. If you're staying at a far-flung resort your airport transfer will be by plane. This is a fantastic way to really grasp the extraordinary geography of the country and take some superb photographs. The whole process is run impeccably, with cars and buses taking you where you need to be exactly at the right time, complimentary food and drinks and a deluxe waiting lounge available some of the time. Two seaplane companies are used for resort transfers. If you wish to travel by seaplane independently, the usual restrictions will apply.

Bike riding is safer away from Male

# Accommodation

*In its attempts to maximise the profits from tourism without opening the floodgates to unchecked development, the Maldivian hospitality industry has chosen to develop only high-end options. The majority of resorts are 4- or 5-star, and outside Male you won't find anywhere ranked lower than 3-star. While the differences between 3- and 4-star accommodation may be subtle, step up to 5-star and you will notice it in both service and facilities – as well as the price, of course.*

Cost is also affected by whether you book directly with a hotel itself or via a travel agent as part of a package tour. The latter is far cheaper. Bear in mind, too, that some resorts grade themselves according to a local scale that is not consistent with international hotel rankings. Before you decide on somewhere, check how the tour operator categorises the resort, as that will give you a better idea of what to expect. There is usually no more than one level of difference between the two rankings.

The reception desk at Angsana, North Male Atoll

At first glance, the Maldives seems an expensive destination, particularly in comparison with nearby countries such as Sri Lanka or India. However, industry standards are far higher in the Maldives. Hotel employees are professional and polite and facilities are kept scrupulously clean. There are also none of the usual fears associated with other destinations in the region, such as theft, poor food hygiene and being ripped off and hassled.

In any case, staying in the Maldives may not be as expensive as its reputation. Going in low season, taking advantage of a last-minute booking and going easy on the extras such as spa treatments and pricy hotel cocktails can all keep the overall cost reasonable.

If you do want to splash out, many resorts offer water bungalows, wooden constructions on stilts built over the sea. Connected to the shore by a pier, they often have ladders going directly down into the water for handy swimming. In larger resorts that offer

A bedroom at the Banyan Tree Resort

both water bungalows and standard accommodation, there is sometimes a separate restaurant so higher-paying guests can eat away from the hoi polloi.

Aside from a water bungalow, if you really want to sleep over the sea, your other option is a boat-based holiday. These range from small chartered vessels, known as safari boats or live-aboards, where you muck in and help the crew prepare the evening meal which they will have plucked from the sea that day, to luxury cruise ships with air-conditioning and Jacuzzis. This is a good choice for anyone who would like to see a bit more of the Maldives, as well as for divers, for whom some boats specifically cater.

The only anomaly, accommodation wise, is Male. Here cheaper options are available, aimed largely at the Sri Lankan and Indian expats who work on the islands. Tourists are still liable for the $8-a-night bed tax, which means that nowhere is going to be dirt cheap. These places are not luxurious but are decent enough if you want to spend a few days in Male on a budget. At the other end of the scale are the upmarket hotels clustered around the airport jetty catering to affluent holidaymakers or business people passing through the capital. The government's determination to keep locals and tourists apart precludes any homestay-style accommodation.

# Food and drink

*If your resort is typical, the food is likely to be one of the high points of your trip. Menus have been thoroughly thought through, with the attention to detail that goes into all aspects of the local tourism industry, and there is plenty of choice and variety. How far this can be said to be representative of Maldivian cooking is another matter. Aside from fish, few foodstuffs come easily to the islands. Coconut is an exception, and, along with rice and fish, is the local staple.*

As with many aspects of Maldivian culture, it would be quite possible to come to the country and leave again without coming into contact with the local cuisine. Resort managers are well aware of the timorous palates of many of their foreign visitors, and hotel buffets are stocked full of European and Far Eastern options. Some places do hold themed Maldivian nights, and these, along with any outings to Male, are likely to be your best options to sample local food, albeit a sanitised version.

## Resort food

Resorts usually serve meals buffet style. Given the logistics involved in importing almost everything, the results are impressive. The vast majority of hotels are rated very highly for their food. There is huge choice, dishes represent a gamut of different countries and continents, and all food is well presented and served up cheerfully by professional staff. Much of it is meaty,

but the sheer number of separate items means that vegetarians should also have a decent range of options. Every meal ends with a selection of tropical fruit. The 5-star resorts of course go the extra mile and provide items such as sushi and seafood delicacies. All resorts offer extraordinary table decorations (such as intricate sculptures from fruit) that add to the atmosphere.

## Local cuisine and customs

Maldivian cuisine has been shaped greatly by the local conditions and restrictions. The land – what little there is of it – is stubbornly resistant to farming. With few animals for meat available (pigs are banned for religious reasons, the lack of pasture precludes too many cows and only a few islands have a small number of goats), fish, in particular tuna, is the main source of protein, largely coupled with imported rice. With homogeny in the food itself, the variety comes from the cooking methods. Fish can be boiled, smoked and left in the sun; barbecued, made into a paste and cooked over a fire; fried; curried; served as a soup; even concentrated – or any combination of the above. Curries are popular, and are not as spicy as you'd find in Sri Lanka or India. Maldivian cuisine does have shared elements with the food of its neighbours, although the fact that its own experience of European settlement was far more limited than theirs means that it lacks the same foreign influences.

A resort chef displays a plate of lobsters

Fridges are a luxury, and with the constant heat, food must be prepared on a daily basis. The Maldives is a traditional, Islamic society, and so cooking usually falls to the women, the majority of whom still use wood-burning stoves. As a result, the kitchen is usually in an outhouse to keep the smoke from entering the rest of the home.

Like Indians, Maldivians eat with their right hands; the left is used for cleaning up after going to the toilet and is therefore considered unclean.

### Fruit and vegetables

Fruit and vegetables are limited, so the small number that there are tend to figure heavily. Coconut, one of a few

A tempting bottle full of fruit on a counter

---

**FOOD LEGENDS**

The two main foodstuffs of the Maldives – coconuts and tuna fish – both have a legend attached. The coconut story is rather macabre. The original settlers of the archipelago are said to have died in their multitudes. But a sorcerer, or *fandita*, was able to conjure coconut trees to grow from the skulls of the interred corpses. This distastefulness is not uncommon in Maldivian folk stories, many of which are full of bodily fluids and functions that have been omitted from their sanitised modern retellings. The supposed origins of tuna are more palatable; it is said a seafarer went to the mythical tree at the end of the world to get the fish and bring it back to Maldives waters.

---

fruits that grow on the islands, plays a significant part in the local diet, as do onions, lime and chillies. Bananas and screw pine are another two home-grown fruits that can be picked up at the market. *Murunga* is the lone green vegetable that flourishes.

### Snacks

The locals are also keen on their *hedhikaa*, or 'short eats'. These are a variety of snacks, often fried pastry with a fish filling, but some are also sweet and others spicy. Given their size, short eats provide a relatively risk-free introduction to the national cuisine. They are on sale in cafés throughout Male. If, despite all the government's efforts to the contrary, you do find yourself invited into a local home, short eats are likely to be dished up there too. They are often served with betel leaves and lime paste.

## Drinks

Alcohol is banned under the country's Sharia law, but the government had to capitulate and make a concession for tourists on resort islands. Waiters are sent on courses to learn all about alcohol, and you may find yourself in the amusing situation of getting wine recommendations from a waiter who has never tasted a drop in his life.

The resorts often have an extensive cocktail menu, and prices will probably be no more than you would pay in the average upmarket bar in London. They also do plenty of refreshing fresh fruit juices and soft drinks. Bottled mineral water rather than tap water should be drunk, as most resort islands have their own desalination plants to provide fresh water.

## Tipping

Tipping is not part of the Maldivian culture, but the advent of so many foreign tourists spending high sums of money on having fun in a country where the average wage is low means that inevitably some expectation now exists. In many resorts little cash is exchanged throughout the holiday, with guests adding all charges to their room account and then going to settle up at reception from time to time or just before departure. This means that tipping is not an issue most of the time. It is acceptable to tip your waiter, if you were served by one in particular, at the end of your trip. If there was no one waiter who provided you with service, you can leave a sum at reception to be distributed among the staff.

There is no problem finding alcohol on the islands

# Entertainment

*Most holidaymakers who come to the Maldives do so in couples, often on honeymoon, so organised entertainment is not high on their list of priorities – peace and quiet are. The Islamic regime means there is no drinking and disco culture in the country. But resorts do make an effort to entertain their guests, with the larger ones putting on some kind of event most evenings. Male also offers the easiest opportunity to see how the Maldivians themselves relax.*

With full-board and all-inclusive deals common, and days spent away from resort islands rare, opportunities to eat and drink in authentic Maldivian establishments are likely to be limited. However, the larger resorts usually have at least one and sometimes several speciality restaurants where diners can have a break from the usual buffet meal and go à la carte. These places are not cheap but the standards are very high – as they have to be if they are going to lure guests away from the buffet meal which they've already paid for – and the hotel often provides extras, such as lobster specials, or serves meals at tables on the beach. More deluxe resorts go even further, giving guests the chance to have a personal chef for the evening, and serving the meal wherever the diners wish, from their own room or terrace to an isolated spot on the island or even a nearby uninhabited island reserved for the purpose.

Other resort entertainment mostly takes the usual forms common to beach destinations. Livelier hotels host discos and karaoke nights. However, turnout is often very low, and on some smaller islands the advertised event rarely goes ahead. Many places hire bands to come and play for a few hours after dinner, either mellow cover versions of songs appropriate for the beach setting (Bob Marley features prominently) or tourist-friendly takes on traditional music.

The most popular type of traditional music is *Bodu Beru* (*see p17*), which is believed to have its origins in East African music. It is also known as *Baburu Lava*, and involves drums, singing, bells and bamboo. Seeing *Bodu Beru* performed live, in its true form, is nigh on impossible for tourists, so the resort versions are generally the closest you'll get to seeing a traditional show. The larger resorts tend to have more comprehensive evening entertainment programmes, and are therefore more likely to offer Maldivian music and dance. Kurumathi, with its three hotels on one island, is one such place. Bigger resorts with a more participatory atmosphere may also include a form of traditional dancing in the show, and eager guests are welcome to join in. Unusually for a smaller island, where guests tend to prefer quiet relaxation to organised activities, Banyan Tree also regularly hosts a local band, as do Dhoni Mighili and Vilu Reef. The *Atoll Explorer* (*see panel, p93*) will provide a taste of traditional culture in something closer to its authentic form, and being on a boat you may at least be able to escape the resort atmosphere, although the show

This is the only opportunity for gambling in the Maldives

will still be tourist-oriented. If the opportunity to see local cultural shows is an important part of your trip, it is worth checking ahead to ensure that your resort stages them.

A slightly more unusual activity – and one that may sit uneasily with Western concepts of animal rights – is crab racing, where guests select a crab that, upon its release from under a glass, 'races' out of a circle against other contenders, with the winning crustacean earning its backer a prize, often some drinks. This is as much action as gamblers are going to get; there are no casinos in the Maldives, although this is something that entrepreneurial hoteliers are hoping will change in the future, and given the Islamic country's concessions to tourism to date, their hopes are not wholly unfounded.

Other options include a sunset sail, where you can enjoy a cocktail on the sea as the sun goes down, magic shows for families and occasional pieces of theatre staged by resorts. But most holidaymakers seem to derive entertainment enough from simply sitting at a table by the sea, sipping on a cocktail, beer or juice.

There are rare exceptions to the laid-back vibe. Resorts close to Male which host cabin crew on their week-long break before the return flight, such as Bandos and Paradise Island, can get more animated, with a group of 20-somethings making the most of their stopover. But generally entertainment is

---

### THE SMOKE-FREE WOMEN OF GURAADHOO

It won't be obvious from the staff at your resort, who will conduct themselves with impeccable professionalism, but Maldivians are heavy smokers, despite a hearty government campaign to stamp it out. A high-profile move in this regard came from the women of Guraadhoo Island, in Thaa Atoll, when the 886 of them quit en masse on annual Non-Smoking Day in 2000. The Guraadhoo's Woman's Committee chairwoman said the impressive feat took two years, with the last recalcitrant a 50-year-old guda-guda (water-pipe) devotee. The committee was aiming to encourage the island's menfolk to follow suit, although no reports of their success subsequently emerged.

---

on the modest side and usually winds up around midnight or 1am.

For a more authentic view of the Maldivian leisure scene, spend some time in Male's cafés and teahouses. Although these are often populated exclusively by local men, foreigners of both sexes are permitted and it can be a good way to meet and talk to Maldivians other than resort staff. Unfortunately, most travellers will see Male only from a distance, upon arrival or departure, or on a day trip, with their return boat taking them back to their resort in time for the evening meal. One of the best times to wander the capital is in the evening, not just to avoid the searing heat, but to witness the Maldivians making the most of the temperature respite, shopping (shops are open until 11pm) or just relaxing and strolling. The town also has a cinema, used generally to show local films, sometimes poor-quality versions of Hollywood hits, and to host local events like competitions and award ceremonies.

Understandably for communities as remote as many Maldivian ones are, the advent of cable television from abroad brought with it a mini-revolution in leisure habits. Hindi soap operas achieved particular success, gathering legions of fans. The more high-brow can be found, often under a shady tree, playing the local version of chess, a faster game with slightly different pieces.

A typical local café in Male

# Shopping

*The Maldives is not blessed with an abundance of natural resources, and travellers hoping to pick up truly local souvenirs may be disappointed as much of the merchandise on sale is likely to have been imported. Efforts to encourage the development of a local handicraft industry are ongoing, although the enforced separation of local people and tourists presents an obvious practical problem. As you'd expect, resort shops stock all the standards – T-shirts, calendars, pens, mugs and so on, all with Maldives emblazoned on them.*

For more authentic souvenirs, there are a couple of branches of handicraft work that could yield results. The coconut tree is the source of many products. Leaves are sewn with coir rope, itself derived from the fibre of coconut husk, to make the *cadjan*, a type of mat. Another mat, the *sataa*, is made from screw pine leaf. Lacquerwork (*see pp15–16*), a complex decorative art for which a lathe is used to produce wooden sticks, games, boxes and other containers is also a common practice, but, as for all crafts, it is difficult to find opportunities to purchase such goods, unless one is organised by the resort. It is easier to pick up stamps, coins and shark jaws (if they are to your taste), or jewellery in your choice of gold, silver, mother-of-pearl and coral. (No black coral or its by-products, and no stony coral, excluding organ pipe coral, can be exported, so check what kind it is before you buy.) Given how switched on Maldivian hoteliers are to all

opportunities to maximise revenues from their business, it seems likely that in the future the local craft industry will be opened up to foreign tourists.

Outside your resort souvenir shop, which can be on the uninspiring side, the best place for shopping is Male. Around the fish market you will find the kind of small stores that yield quirky souvenirs. Unlike the neighbouring countries, there is no real bargaining culture in the Maldives, and you will normally have to pay the marked price. At the other end of the scale are the upmarket, air-conditioned designer stores showcasing global brands.

For duty-free shopping, the facilities at Male International Airport are highly regarded, and seem more suited to a Western capitalist state than a small Islamic nation in Asia. The shopping section is bright and clean, with a range of stores selling clothes, souvenirs, alcohol, perfume, luxury goods, electronics, watches, toys, books and food. Prices are given in American dollars. Ironically, given the futility of trying to bargain elsewhere in Male, it can sometimes be worth trying for a discount.

Many shops in the Maldives now accept credit cards; your resort store almost certainly will, and you should be able to charge any items to your room and pay at the end. Of course, smaller, local stores will not have credit card facilities, but it is nearly always possible to pay in dollars rather than in rufiyaa. Shops may seem to have rather bizarre opening times, closing up to five times a day. This is because of Muslim prayer time. However, they do stay open late, to around 11pm in Male.

When making your purchase decisions, bear in mind that taking some types of coral, pearl oyster and turtle shell products out of the country is strictly prohibited.

A souvenir shop in Angsana

# Sport and leisure

*While traditional ways to pass the time on a beach holiday may be lacking in the Maldives, when it comes to aquatic activities the country more than makes amends. Whether it's as adventurous as scuba-diving or as tame as doing a few lengths in the hotel pool, the majority of holidaymakers spend a significant amount of their trip in the water, or on it; boat trips for fishing, cocktails or whale-watching are also a popular activity.*

## Boating

There are plenty of boat trips and activities to satisfy all designs from the romantic to the exploratory and even predatory. The most relaxing trip is probably the sunset sails offered by many resorts, where you're served a cocktail and float around as darkness falls. If normal boats are too mundane for your taste, you can also head out to sea in a submarine (*see p148*).

For a bit more excitement, there is also whale and dolphin spotting. The Maldives Tourism Promotion Board boasts that the country is among the top five places for watching these mammals in the world, being home to more than 20 different species.

As well as the organised trips, which go out in the morning and afternoon, you may even be lucky and spot some by chance on an unrelated boat trip; the crew will happily make a diversion in pursuit. The odd shark fin can also sometimes be seen gliding menacingly in and out of the water.

The unsqueamish can go fishing for big game, and your catch will be cooked and served upon your return.

## Diving

Aside from honeymooners, scuba-divers are perhaps the other main group who come to the Maldives. Peak diving season, for the clarity of the sea, runs from January to April, coinciding with the general holiday season, although there are alternative advantages, such as the larger fish being more active, throughout the rest of the year. Diving is covered in more depth in the special feature (*see pp94–5*).

## Fish feeding

Vegans, animal lovers and anyone else who would rather feed the fish than kill them will enjoy the fish feeding that takes place on a few islands. Although the ethics of this are a divisive issue among environmentalists and marine biologists, it certainly makes a fascinating spectacle, with a resort employee sticking his food-filled hand into the mouths of stingrays and manta rays in what looks like a perilous manoeuvre, while guests gather round on the jetty with their cameras.

## Land sports

Back on land there are also plenty of ways to pass the time. Anxious to prevent their customers from getting bored and booking shorter trips, hoteliers facilitate a range of activities for every level of energy from snooker, pool and darts to table tennis, tennis, squash, badminton and fitness. Many islands have well-equipped gyms. At larger resorts you might even find a golf course. Beaches commonly have volleyball nets, although these are rarely used until the sun begins to set. The locals' first love is football. Incredibly, for such a small island, Male alone is said to have as many as 40 clubs. Resort staff defy the heat to have a kick-around most days. Larger islands even have small leagues which may see the waiters take on the front-of-house staff or the cleaners. Guests sometimes get to watch or join in too. Maldivians are very proud of their national side's efforts. More information is available at *www.famaldives.gov.mv*

A jet-ski being pushed up the beach at Paradise Island

## Snorkelling

Anyone who likes the idea of seeing the underwater world but finds oxygen tanks too intimidating can start with snorkelling. Mask, breathing tube and flippers (or fins to the snorkelling *cognoscenti*) can be hired from your resort, usually for around $10 a day, although more expensive hotels may allow guests free use. If you plan to do a lot of snorkelling, it may be worth investing in your own gear before you leave home or in Male. Courses are available but it's easy enough to pick up the basics by yourself, and the staff at the diving school are generally happy to give beginners a few pointers. Once you've got the hang of it – best done in shallower areas as it may involve some unpleasant mouthfuls of seawater while you master the apparatus – the reef edges offer the richest range of fish.

## Spas

Outdoor aerobic activity can quickly lose its allure in 30°C (86°F) heat, and many visitors are looking for a more relaxing pastime, which resorts increasingly provide with a large spa menu. While the Maldives might not have the homegrown ayurveda tradition of India and Sri Lanka, that has not stopped it developing a network of spas catering largely to the stressed-out European and Asian executives recharging their batteries on the islands. These are typically very professional outlets, with highly trained therapists brought in from the Philippines, Thailand and Malaysia.

Everything from a 20-minute head massage to a week-long treatment programme is available. Nothing is cheap, but it shouldn't cost more than an equivalent therapeutic service in your home country, and the environment and service are both impeccable.

## Water sports

Apart from diving and snorkelling, other water sports are on hand by the bucket load, although resort managers are well aware that the majority of guests come in search of serenity, so you won't find jetskiiers noisily zooming up and down just off the beach, as you might in more boisterous Indian Ocean resorts such as Goa, for example. The geography of the islands makes the surrounding lagoons good starting points for novices, protected as they are from the choppier waters. Windsurfing and canoeing are possible pretty much everywhere, with surfing possible at points in North Male Atoll and at the southern end of the country. Unlike the majority of tourists, surfers positively welcome the blustery weather of the monsoon, which can whip up waves of up to 2m (6$^{1}/_{2}$ft) high.

The noisier water sports, such as jetskiing, waterskiing, wakeboarding, kneeboarding, parasailing and banana boating, are not as ubiquitous, but they can be found at those resorts where it is possible to offer them without disturbing the rest of the guests. Depending on your level of proficiency, you may be allowed to rent the equipment and head off alone, but you are expected to stay within certain areas from where you can be seen from the shore in case of an emergency. Resorts have strict procedures in place to reduce chances of an accident. Security and lifeguards (or signs to warn you if they are not present) keep track of guests doing water sports out at sea, and many hotels are increasing their emergency facilities, introducing decompression chambers and the like.

A water sports centre on Sun Island

# Children

*It's not the obvious place to take children, but the Maldives has plenty to amuse younger visitors. Hoteliers are aware that their guests, predominantly couples, will probably prefer a holiday without too many children tearing through the restaurant and leaping into the pool, and kids' clubs are not the norm. Some resorts go so far as to ban younger children. But the endless enjoyment children derive from the beach and the huge sense of security parents get from the resort-island set-up can be the basis for a fun family holiday.*

The Maldives' credentials as a family-friendly destination are evident: no traffic or busy roads (excluding Male); self-contained resorts where comings and goings are monitored and everyone is either staff member or guest; ubiquitous security guards and lifeguards; and of course clean golden sand and safe lagoon swimming. Snorkelling is likely to be the top activity for all but the very youngest children, who are often catered for in a children's pool. Apart from the no-children resorts, most other places make some effort to entertain kids. Reflecting Maldivians' general child-friendliness, resort employees are happy to amuse young visitors as much as they can, although official entertainment – with the exception of the odd magic show and fish-feeding – is mostly aimed at adult guests.

A main deterrent for budget-conscious families is the expense. In high season the Maldives is a pricey destination, and travelling in a large family group, particularly with older children with a big appetite for water sports, could greatly ratchet up the cost.

## Practicalities

Many hotels have some interconnected rooms or bungalows that cater for family groups, although it's worth double-checking any request for this in the run-up to departure, as resorts often reach full occupancy in high season and if your request has been overlooked the situation may not be easy to rectify. Hotel shops might stock nappies, but choice is likely to be limited, so it's worth bringing such provisions with you. Some resorts offer a baby-sitting service. Food hygiene is not a concern here. Scrupulous standards are observed in the serving and preparation of meals, and there will be a good choice of items from your home cuisine. High chairs will be provided, serving staff

A boy having fun in a Paradise Island pool

will happily chop up food for children and the genuine perma-smiles of staff will not slip if your toddler starts acting up.

If problems arise, they are likely to stem from the hot weather and the long flight which, at around 11 hours from the UK, tests even adult patience. For more serious complaints, larger islands have on-site doctors and/or medical centres, although protective parents may prefer to choose a resort that is not too far from Male, in case of an emergency.

## Safety

As anywhere, children require supervision when in the water. While the lagoon provides generally safe swimming conditions, treading on the coral can be very painful, and although the water is mostly free from nasties, if you stand still long enough a curious fish may attempt a nibble. There'll be no lasting damage but it's not pleasant for children. Reef sharks – though they rarely concern themselves with swimmers – could also alarm young swimmers.

# Essentials

## Arriving and departing

All tourists going to the Maldives will arrive by plane, mostly on long-haul flights, and the vast majority will be on a package holiday. It is possible to book flights and accommodation separately, but this increases both the price and the hassle. All major travel agents offer packages to the Maldives, with flights from the UK departing from Gatwick and Manchester.

If you don't want to go for a package deal, Sri Lanka is the only scheduled airline to operate non-stop flights, but on the way back you will have to change in Colombo. Various other airlines offer services from Europe with a stopover.

For anyone who has travelled throughout the region, Male International Airport will come as a pleasant surprise. Small and easily navigable, it's efficiently run, clean and mercifully free of the legions of taxi drivers/luggage porters/assorted others who assail you in, say, Delhi. There's a decent array of shops and facilities, a 24-hour information desk and a marvellous Swiss ice cream parlour. Resort and travel agent desks staffed by reps are lined up in two rows facing each other to assist weary and bewildered passengers.

## Customs

Don't attempt to circumvent the Maldives' ban on the sale of alcohol by bringing your own supply. Importing it is not allowed either and it will be seized upon arrival. A few other items are also forbidden under the country's religious law: anything offensive to Islam (in effect pornography and idols but, to be on the safe side, your holiday reading matter should probably not include *The Satanic Verses*); drugs; and live pigs or pork and its by-products. Customs rules permit passengers to bring in a small quantity of tobacco, cigarettes or cigars. Any amount of currency, both foreign and local, can be taken in or out without restriction. In theory, video tapes must be handed over to customs for approval by government censors. Further up-to-date information is available at *www.customs.gov.mv*

## Electricity

Your hotel room sockets are likely to come in several permutations, so both continental European and British appliances should work without problem. Take a multi-adaptor if you have one. The electricity supply, which comes from generators on each island at an output of 220–240V, is generally reliable, although on inhabited (non-resort) islands it may be restricted to the evening.

## Internet

Most if not all resort islands offer public internet access, sometimes directly from each hotel room, sometimes in a cyber café. However, the connection can be maddeningly slow, and the prices high. The cyber cafés in Male are slightly better.

## Money

The Maldivian currency is the rufiyaa, one of which is made up of 100 laari. Notes come in denominations of Rf2, Rf5, Rf10, Rf20, Rf50, Rf100 and Rf500. Coins have values of 1, 5, 10, 25 and 50 laari and 1 and 2 rufiyaa. However, many visitors come and go and never see local money. Resorts price everything in US dollars and American currency is also accepted in Male and some inhabited islands. The exchange rate is pegged at Rf12.75, so there's no advantage in shopping around. Cashing traveller's cheques incurs a charge of up to 5 per cent. If you want to change money your best bet is to go to one of the banks in Male. They usually have ATMs, most of which will take foreign cards. Credit card acceptance is widespread in hotels, restaurants and tourist shops although smaller outlets may lack the necessary facilities.

A tranquil evening on Royal Island jetty

A display at the Aaramu Spa in Royal Island resort

### Opening hours

The main bane for tourists is prayer time, for which shops close five times a day. Otherwise, opening hours for shops are 8am–8pm or sometimes 11pm. On Friday they open at about 1.30pm. Banks operate 9am–1pm but remain closed on Friday.

### Passports and visas

Advance visas are not required for stays of less than a month, but your passport must be valid for at least six months from your arrival date. Extensions for the visa stamped into your passport on your arrival can be sought at the Department of Immigration.
*Ground floor, Huravee Building, Ameer Ahmed Magu. Tel: 333 0444.*

*www.immigration.gov.mv.*
*Open: Sun–Thur 7.30am–2.30pm.*

### Pharmacies

There are no pharmacies on the resort islands. Your resort shop may stock basic provisions, but Male is the best option for pharmacies. One, at the ADK Hospital on Sosun Magu, is open 24 hours.

### Post

A standard postcard sent by airmail costs Rf10, a larger one or a letter Rf12. They are likely to reach their destination in around seven to ten days. Resort shops sell stamps and will post letters for you. Male has several post offices and there is one at the airport if you've left the postcards to the last minute.

## Public holidays

With the exception of a few festivals on fixed Western dates, the remaining public holidays are Islamic and determined by the lunar calendar, and therefore change from year to year. The dates below are for 2008.

**January**
1 New Year's Day
10 Islamic New Year

**March**
20 Mawlid al-Nabi (Birth of the Prophet)

**April**
27 National Day
The Day Maldives Embraced Islam (date to be confirmed)

**July**
26–27 Independence Day

**September**
2 Ramadan begins

**October**
2 Eid al-Fitr (Ramadan ends)

**November**
3 Victory Day
11 Republic Day

**December**
9 Eid al-Adha (Feast of the Sacrifice)

10 Fisheries Day
29 Islamic New Year
Hajj Day (to be confirmed)

## Smoking

While Maldivians, particularly the men, are keen smokers, you will rarely see a resort employee with a cigarette in hand. Large resorts sometimes have separate smoking and non-smoking sections in their restaurants, but the majority of holidaymakers are non-smokers. Restaurants are well ventilated and often open-air or at least open at the sides, so cigarette smoke is likely to remain no more than a minor irritation in any case.

## Suggested reading and media

Academic Andrew Forbes' book *Maldives: Kingdom of a Thousand Isles* is a delightful compendium of information, history, nature, literature and personal anecdotes, put together

### FRANÇOIS PYRARD DE LAVAL

Frenchman François Pyrard de Laval was sailing from his home country to the East Indies in 1602 when he was shipwrecked on a Maldivian reef. He and several of the crew of the *Corbin* were seized, and Pyrard spent five years in captivity in Male. He did not waste the time, however, and set about learning the local language, which resulted in his associating with the sultan and his court. The sultan's wives were surprised to hear from him that the French king had only one wife. But Pyrard was not enamoured with what he saw, calling the Maldivians 'cunning' and the women 'lewd'. After his rescue, he earned fame from a journal of his experiences.

A windsurfer in action at Paradise Island

over some 30 years of visiting the islands. Neville Coleman broaches the gargantuan topic *Marine Life of the Maldives*, illustrated with over 1,000 colour photographs. A glossary at the back ensures the layman can get something out of it too. And a French explorer catalogues his experiences during five years of captivity in 17th-century Male (*see panel, p137*) in *The Voyage of François Pyrard of Laval: To the East Indies, the Maldives, the Moluccas, and Brazil.*

Most tourists use their time in the Maldives to get away from it all, but if you do want to stay in touch with current affairs, the easiest way is probably the television in your hotel room, which should have CNN if not BBC World. If you have a radio you may also be able to pick up the BBC World Service. Some

local daily newspapers have English-language sections, and the *International Herald Tribune* reaches some resorts.

**Tax**

The $8 bed tax and $12 departure tax should be included in the price of your holiday or flight.

**Telephones**

Telecommunication infrastructure has gone from zero to today's modern service in a few short decades. IDD calls from landlines are not cheap, and calls from your hotel room even less so. Roaming is available so you can use your home mobile, although reception can be patchy if you try to do so on some boat trips.

To call the Maldives from abroad, dial the international code (usually 00) followed by the country code (960) and the local number. There are no area codes in the Maldives.

## Time
The Maldives is five hours ahead of GMT, nine hours ahead of Eastern Standard Time, three ahead of South Africa, seven behind New Zealand and five behind Australia. Because it's on the equator there is no daylight saving, so in countries that do adjust their clocks the time difference will vary by an hour depending on the timing of the trip.

## Toilets
Resort toilets are free, Western style, spotless and fully equipped. Elsewhere, loo paper may be lacking, so it's a good idea to carry some tissues just in case.

## Travellers with disabilities
With no busy roads, reckless drivers or even non-reckless drivers,

Maldivian resorts are among the best equipped for disabled travellers in the region. The restriction on building any higher than the tallest palm tree means that most accommodation is on the ground floor, and many rooms are also spacious and ideal for wheelchairs. Inform your hotel in advance of your needs and they will be able to provide ramps if necessary.

Resort employees are professional, customer-oriented and always happy to assist. One difficulty may be the surface of pathways, which, in resorts' attempts to harmonise with nature, are sometimes rough-hewn. Another will be Male, where bad paving, narrow streets and alarming drivers make it all but impossible for anyone with restricted mobility. If you're determined to see it, the best idea is probably to do so by taxi.

A school sign on a village island in North Male Atoll

# Language

English is widely spoken in the Maldives, and you would have to be a very long way off the beaten track to find yourself somewhere with no English speakers. Dhivehi, the local language, is not easy for the foreigner to master. If you attempt it, remember to emphasise the first syllable of each word. Some ideas, such as 'thank you', tend to be expressed physically rather than enunciated.

## USEFUL DHIVEHI PHRASES

| | |
|---|---|
| **Hello (formal)** | Assalaamu Alaikum |
| **Hello (informal)** | Kihineh? |
| **How are you?** | Haalu kihineh? |
| **Yes** | Aan |
| **No** | Noon |
| **There** | Ethaa |
| **Here** | Mithaa |
| **This** | Mi |
| **That** | E |
| **Good** | Ran'galhu |
| **Thank you** | Shukuriyaa |
| **I am sorry** | Ma-aafu kurey |
| **Goodbye (informal)** | Dhanee |

## QUESTIONS AND ANSWERS

| | |
|---|---|
| **Where?** | Kobaa? |
| **Why?** | Keevve? |
| **Who?** | Kaaku? |
| **What?** | Koacheh? |
| **What is (your) name?** | Kon nameh kiyanee? |
| **My name is** | Aharenge namakee |
| **How old are you?** | Umurun kihaa vareh? |
| **My age is** | Aharenge umurakee … |
| **Where are you from?** | Kon rasheh? |
| **What is the price?** | Agu kihaavareh? |
| **How long will it take?** | Kihaa ireh nagaanee? |
| **What time is it?** | Gadin kihaa ireh? |
| **What island is that?** | E-ee kon rasheh? |

## NUMBERS

| | |
|---|---|
| 0 | Sumeh |
| 1 | Ekeh |
| 2 | Dheyh |
| 3 | Thineh |
| 4 | Hathareh |
| 5 | Faheh |
| 6 | Haeh |
| 7 | Hatheh |
| 8 | Asheh |
| 9 | Nuvaeh |
| 10 | Dhihaeh |
| 20 | Vihi |
| 30 | Thirees |
| 40 | Saalhees |
| 50 | Fansaan |
| 60 | Fasdholhas |
| 70 | Hadhdhiha |
| 80 | Addiha |
| 90 | Nuvadhiha |
| 100 | Satheyka |
| 1,000 | Enhaas |

## DAYS AND TIMES

| | |
|---|---|
| **Friday** | Hukuru |
| **Saturday** | Honihiru |
| **Sunday** | Aaditta |
| **Monday** | Hoama |
| **Tuesday** | Angaara |
| **Wednesday** | Budha |
| **Thursday** | Buraasfati |
| **Yesterday** | Iyye |
| **Today** | Miadhu |
| **Tomorrow** | Maadhan |
| **Morning** | Hendhunu |
| **Midday** | Mendhuru |
| **Night** | Reygandu |
| **Hour** | Gadi |
| **Day** | Dhuvas |
| **Week** | Hafthaa |
| **Month** | Mas |
| **Year** | Aharu |

## THE CONVERSION OF A NATION

The story goes that a sea demon called Rannamaari was terrorising Male. Each month he demanded a virgin girl be brought to him at a temple, where she would be found violated and dead the following morning. One day an Arab traveller, Abu al-Barakat al-Barbari, came upon the island. He offered to take the place of the next girl. There are different versions of the tale, but the gist of it is that the Arab spent the night reading the Koran, and Rannamaari fled for good, whereupon the king converted the country to Islam.

# Emergencies

## Emergency numbers

Police *119*
Fire *118*
Ambulance *102*

## Medical services

On Male, the public Indira Gandhi Memorial Hospital (*Kanbaa Aisa Rani Hingun, tel: 331 6647*) and private ADK Hospital (*Sosun Magu, tel: 331 3553*) should be your ports of call in an emergency. The latter also has a dental surgery and a 24-hour pharmacy. Pharmacies are fairly plentiful throughout the city, but take any prescription medications, as the resorts are not so well stocked.

If you have small children or a medical condition, you may decide to choose a resort with a resident doctor and health centre. Some are also equipped with decompression chambers for divers.

The logistical costs of reaching the capital in an emergency make taking out adequate insurance essential.

## Health risks

Compared with other destinations in the Indian subcontinent, the Maldives is a picnic health-wise. Malaria has practically been eradicated, although it is still wise to use repellent and cover up in loose light-coloured clothes after dark. Bottled water is advisable, but the tap variety is fine for cleaning your teeth. Food hygiene in the resorts is second to none. If you use common sense, it is normally fine in Male and the villages as well.

Inoculations against diphtheria, tetanus, polio, typhoid and hepatitis A are recommended but not required. They take at least two weeks to take effect.

## Police, safety and crime

With a population of devout, law-abiding Muslims, and small resort islands with controlled populations of employees and guests, the Maldives is a wonderfully safe destination. Few hotels report any problems with theft (but don't be careless with your valuables), and scams perpetrated on tourists are unheard of. Prison conditions are the subject of controversy in the country, but unless you try to smuggle in alcohol or drugs, this is unlikely to affect you. Male's traffic can be hazardous; pay attention at all times.

The greatest safety issue is the sea. Lagoon swimming is usually safe, and many resorts have security guards monitoring bathers, but pay attention to any signs and be warned that currents can form close to islands. The heat may also affect those unused to it, and the usual advice applies: keep hydrated; wear sun cream and a hat; wear a T-shirt if you're snorkelling; and seek shade during the hottest hours.

## Embassies and consulates

### Australia
*Australian High Commission in Sri Lanka. 21 Gregory's Road, Colombo 7. Tel: (94) (11) 246 3200.*

### Canada
*Canadian High Commission in Sri Lanka. 6 Gregory's Road, Colombo 7. Tel: (94) (11) 522 6232.*

### New Zealand
*Honorary Consul in Male, Mr Ahmed Saleem. C/- Crown Company Pvt Ltd, 30H Sea Coast, Boduthakurufaanu Magu. Tel: 332 2432.*

*New Zealand High Commission in Singapore. Ngee Ann City, Tower A, 15-06/10, 391A Orchard Road. Tel: (65) 6235 9966.*

### South Africa
*South African High Commission in New Delhi. B18 Vasant Marg Vasant Vihar. Tel: (91) (11) 2614 9411 ext 19.*

### UK
*British Consular Correspondent in Male. Tel: 311 218.*

*British Embassy in Sri Lanka. 190 Galle Road, Kollupitiya, Colombo 3. Tel: (94) (11) 243 7336 ext 43.*

### USA
*American Embassy in Sri Lanka. 210 Galle Road, Colombo 3. Tel: (94) (11) 249 8500.*

## Maldivian consulates, embassies and high commissions abroad

### Australia
*Consulate-General of the Republic of Maldives, 164 Gatehouse Street, Parkville, Victoria 3052. Tel: (03) 9349 1473. Fax: (03) 9349 1119. linton@iimetro.com.au*

### Canada
Apply to the Embassy in the USA.

### New Zealand
There is no Maldivian representation here.

### South Africa
*Honorary Consul of the Republic of Maldives, 69 Totnis Road, Plumstead, Cape Town. Tel: (021) 797 9940. Fax: (086) 640 2037.*

### UK
*High Commission of Maldives, 22 Nottingham Place, Marylebone, London W1U 5NJ. Tel: (44) 020 7224 2135. Fax: (44) 020 7224 2157. maldives.high.commission@virgin.net*

### USA
*Embassy of the Republic of Maldives, Suite 400 E, 800, Second Avenue, New York NY 10017. Tel: (212) 599 6194. Fax: (212) 599 6195. info@maldives.un.int*

Emergencies

# Directory

## Accommodation price guide

Prices are based on a double room per night for two people, with breakfast, in high season. Low season prices may be significantly reduced, and booking directly with a hotel will be much more expensive than going with a travel agent.

| | |
|---|---|
| ★ | under $150 |
| ★★ | $150–300 |
| ★★★ | $300–550 |
| ★★★★ | over $550 |

## Eating out price guide

Prices are based on an average three-course meal for one, without drinks.

| | |
|---|---|
| ★ | under $20 |
| ★★ | $20–40 |
| ★★★ | $40–80 |
| ★★★★ | over $80 |

## Male

Male hotels and restaurants are on a different scale, and require their own price ranking.

| Accommodation | | Eating out | |
|---|---|---|---|
| ★ under $50 | | ★ under $7 | |
| ★★ $50–80 | | ★★ $7–10 | |
| ★★★ $80–150 | | ★★★ $10–15 | |
| ★★★★ over $150 | | ★★★★ over $15 | |

### MALE

#### ACCOMMODATION

**Buruneege Residence ★**
Very close to all the main points of interest in Male, this budget guest house offers convenience and good value for money. It has some stylish touches, like the traditional wood of the reception area, and rooms are clean and modern with en suite bathroom and air-conditioning. The garden café is open until late.
*Hithaffiniva Magu.*
*Tel: 333 0011.*
*Email: buruneege@ frontline.com.mv.*
*www.frontline.com.mv*

**Transit Inn ★**
Small and friendly guest house, just south of the centre and all the main attractions. Its garden café, Jugwy's, enjoys a refreshingly green location. Rooms come with fan or air-conditioning.
*Ma Dheyliaage and Maaveyo Magu.*
*Tel: 332 0420.*
*Email: transit@ dhivehinet.net.mv*

**Relax Inn ★★**
Calling itself the tallest hotel in Male, Relax Inn offers great views, and some rooms come with a balcony to best enjoy them. It has an à la carte restaurant on the sixth floor.
*Ameer Ahmed Magu.*
*Tel: 331 4531.*
*Email: hotelrelaxinn@ relaxmaldives.com.*
*www.relaxmaldives.com*

**Villingili View Inn ★★**
Striking a more traditional note in a city whose hotels – along with the rest of its amenities – seem to be striving to be ever more modern is the Villingili View Inn, the best choice of the establishments to the west of Male. Wood has been used extensively throughout the property to give it a pleasant, rustic ambience. The in-house Raaveriya restaurant enjoys an attractive garden and plenty of shade from the trees.
*M Raaverige, Majeedhee Magu. Tel: 332 1135.*

**Central Hotel ★★★**
Bright and cheerful hotel housed in a contemporary building that looks like an office block. Some rooms have balconies and there is a good range of food, but no air-conditioning.
*G Sanoaraage, Rahdhebai Magu. Tel: 331 7766. Email: central@ dhivehinet.net.mv. www.centralmaldives.com*

**Mookai Hotel ★★★**
With a rooftop pool, the Koimala Restaurant on the ninth floor and a café just below on the eighth, this new hotel is close to the airport jetty and a convenient choice if you're short on time. Considering the quality and the facilities, it is not overpriced, and it has excellent views of the city and water.
*H Maagala, 2 Meheli Goalhi. Tel: 333 8811. Email: mookai@ dhivehinet.net.mv*

**Hulhule Island Hotel ★★★★**
Just one minute from the airport in the free minibus shuttle, this bright hotel is the best place to stay if you're flying in late or flying out early. Set in some pleasant gardens overlooking the sea, it has two pools (one for children) and a brand new spa and gym to relieve any traveller's tension. Rooms are modern and attention to detail has gone into all the facilities. The staff are professional and friendly.
*Hulhule Island. Tel: 333 0888. Email: sales@hih.com.mv. www.hih.com.mv*

**EATING OUT**

**Shell Beans ★★**
Highly reputed seafront café with good light lunches, snacks and desserts and fine coffee. It's a small place, the service is efficient and the prices decent.
*Boduthakurufaanu Magu. Tel: 333 3686.*

**Thai Wok ★★**
A Male legend that has spawned lesser imitators, Thai Wok is justifiably popular, and it's worth arriving early or booking ahead to be certain of getting seated. Portions are generous and the food is top quality. Despite being one of the more upmarket eateries on the island, prices remain a bargain. Service is friendly but can be slow.
*Ameer Ahmed Magu. Tel: 3311 0007.*

**Olive Garden ★★★**
Simply but pleasantly decorated with plants and pictures, this place is very popular with tourists, as well as the wealthier locals. There is a wide range of choices, all of which are more than reasonably priced.

*Fareedhee Magu.*
*Tel: 331 2231.*

**Salsa Royal ★★★**
Formerly called Twin Peaks, Salsa Royal is one of the capital's best-known restaurants. Drawing inspiration from various cuisines, including Thai food and pizza, the portions are large and the dining room is well air-conditioned.
*Orchid Magu.*
*Tel: 332 7830.*

**Seagull Café ★★★**
Relaxed eatery with sandy floors, a covered garden and the atmosphere of a beach hut. There is no air-conditioning, but plenty of fans. As well as Asian and European dishes they offer a selection of Italian ice-creams, milkshakes, tea and juices.
*Fareedhee Magu.*
*Tel: 332 3792.*

**Symphony Restaurant ★★★**
Very highly rated restaurant that sees a lot of foreign customers. The temperature is cool, the ambience sophisticated and the fish top-rate. Symphony is one of a chain of three, with similarly named sister restaurants Symphonic (a quality venue that forms part of the Maagiri Tourist Lodge Hotel) and Synthiana (much brighter than the other two) on Boduthakurufaanu Magu and Ameene Magu respectively.
*Athamaa Goalhi.*
*Tel: 332 6277.*

**Faru Coffee House ★★★★**
Bright and relaxed 24-hour café and restaurant with wicker chairs, air-conditioning and a view of the garden. It serves European, Japanese, Italian, Asian and international à la carte dishes, with a buffet over the weekend. The quality of the food meets international hotel standards, and with the highest-priced item $20, it represents great value for money.
*Hulhule Island Hotel, Hulhule Island.*
*Tel: 333 0888.*
*Email: sales@hih.com.mv.*
*www.hih.com.mv*

**ENTERTAINMENT**

**Esjehi Art Gallery**
Housed in a building that dates back to the 1870s – something of a rarity in Male, where such remnants have usually made way for modern blocks – the gallery is worth a visit in its own right, thanks to its beautiful wooden interior. The works exhibited inside, by Maldivian artists, are for sale. The establishment also houses a charming little café. Near the jetty area, it makes an agreeable stop at the end of a tiring boat journey.
*Medhuziyaarai Magu.*
*Tel: 332 0288.*

**National Library and British Council**
Neither of these would normally qualify as typical entertainment in a holiday destination. But in a place where so much of the authentic life is kept outside of the reach of the tourist, the National Library can provide access, of a sort, to Maldivian history, stocking books in English, Dhivehi, Arabic and Urdu, as well as reports, newspaper articles and pamphlets.

*59 Majeedhee Magu.*
*Open: daily 8.15am–9pm,*
*during Ramadan*
*9am–7pm.*

**Olympus Cinema**

The state-run cinema
hosts locally made,
Bollywood and Western
films, although picture
quality is not always
high. More interesting
are the occasional
foreign film festivals and
events. Tickets start from
around $2.

*Majeedhee Magu, opposite*
*the National Stadium.*

**Red Zanzibar**

In the former home of
Haruge (the MDP
meeting-point), this venue
is one of the hippest in
Male, and given the lack
of competition (the
complete absence of
nightclubs, for example)
it is perennially popular.
Look out in particular for
the occasional live jazz
nights. Otherwise, it
consists of an open
restaurant upstairs and
one of the city's nicer
internet cafés downstairs.
Male doesn't get any
closer to nightlife.

*Boduthakurufaanu*
*Magu, opposite the*
*artificial beach.*

## SPORT AND LEISURE

### Diving

**Sea Explorers Dive School**

Male's first dive school
runs services on several
live-aboards, as well as
organising sorties to the
top sites throughout
North and South Male
Atolls. The staff are
flexible, professional and
efficient. Options range
from introductory dives
to professional courses,
and prices are
reasonable.

*1st floor, H Asfaam,*
*Bodufungadhu Magu.*
*Tel: 331 6172. Email:*
*info@seamaldives.com.mv.*
*www.seamaldives.com.mv*

### Football

**Rasmee Dhandu Stadium**

The country's national
stadium hosts primarily
football matches in the
Dhivehi League, FAM
Cup and Male League,
and international
matches, as well as
netball and other
sporting contests. It has
a capacity of just under
12,000. There is no
online or telephone
booking system; it's just
a case of going along on

the day if you hear of a
match taking place.

*Between Majeedhee Magu*
*and Mirihi Magu.*

### Spas

**Hulhule Island Hotel Spa**

The new spa, which
opened in 2007, at the
airport hotel is well
placed for anyone who's
just come off or is just
about to board a long-
haul flight. The serene
two-level facility,
decorated in a simple,
calm-inducing style, is
staffed by a team of
demure masseuses from
the Philippines. There's
a Jacuzzi, sauna and
steam room, plus four
treatment rooms,
including one for couples.

*Hulhule Island Hotel,*
*Hulhule Island.*
*Tel: 333 0888. Email:*
*sales@hih.com.mv.*
*www.hih.com.mv*

**Sheri Saloon**

With the very promising
tagline, 'for the shape of
perfection', yoga, gym,
aerobics classes and
massage are available at
this health centre. You
can also pick up beauty
products and herbal
medicine.

H Rab'ee Manzil, Sosun Magu. Tel: 331 0310. Email: sheri@dhivehinet.net.mv

## Submarine

### Whale Submarine

This submarine ride takes you on a 45-minute journey down 40m (130ft) to the sea bed, with a stop half way down, the idea being to showcase the marine life previously only accessible to scuba-divers. Designed and built in Germany, the sub has reportedly made over 2,000 dives without incident.
Tel: 333 3939. Email: tsub@dhivehinet.net.mv. www.submarinesmaldives.com.mv

## NORTH MALE ATOLL

### ACCOMMODATION

### Asdu Sun Island ★

A resort with one of the most valid claims of offering an authentic Maldivian experience. The décor features coconut fibre, and there is no television, air-conditioning or hot water. With just 30 rooms, it has that lazy island feel, and is the perfect antidote for anyone who spots the inconsistency in getting away from it all to a tropical paradise and then watching CNN on a plasma TV. It will not suit anyone after out-and-out luxury, but provides low-budget relaxation.
Tel: 664 5051. Email: info@asdu.com. www.asdu.com

### Giravaru ★

Giravaru was closed for extensive renovation in August 2007, and was a popular choice even beforehand. The closest low-budget resort to Male, it is popular among backpacking types seeking something other than the everything-laid-on-for-you experience that is typical of Maldivian resorts, and is probably the preferred hotel for independent travellers after Equator Village in Gan. This is a very small and intimate resort, with an excellent house reef close by, and a personalised level of service that can be missing from more upmarket, slicker operators.
Tel: 664 0440. Email: giravaru@dhivehinet.net.mv. www.giravaru.com

### Bandos ★★

Offering tropical island surroundings but with a busier vibe, Bandos is a large island, with 225 rooms and what passes in the Maldives as heavy traffic. Not only does it play host to air crews, whose post-flight partying can be on the frenetic side, but it also gets day-trippers from Male as well as from other resorts that include it on their island-hopping excursions. There is plenty to do, even for children – unusual in the couple-oriented Maldives.
Tel: 664 0088. Email: sales@bandos.com.mv. www.bandos.com.mv

### Kurumba Maldives ★★

The country's first ever holiday resort has not suffered from the competition that has been springing up almost ever since it first opened its doors in October 1972; it has continued to hold its own and retain its fans. Everywhere are touches of class, including a fountain in reception, two-storey presidential suites and a superb aquatic-themed spa. Its proximity to the capital and extensive conference facilities make it a favourite of business travellers.

*Tel: 664 2324. Email: kurumba@dhivehi.net.mv. www.universalresorts.com*

### Paradise Island ★★

A large, luxuriant island with warm, courteous staff and a long beach where isolation and relaxation are guaranteed. The constant presence of flight crews on their stopover makes this one of the livelier islands, with an excellent band making regular appearances and plenty of other entertainment.

*Tel: 664 0011. Email: info@paradise-island.com.mv. www.villahotels.com*

### Thulhaagiri ★★

An understated resort that has managed to retain an authentic village feel. The dense foliage guarantees privacy, as do the palm trees on the beach itself, some of which emerge from the sand at an almost horizontal angle. Highlights of the island are the buffet, which is great, and the birdhouses fixed in the trees outside the reception, home to a colony of brilliantly coloured parrots that are quite wonderful to behold.

*Tel: 664 5930. Email: reserve@ thulhaagiri.com.mv. www.thulhaagiri.com*

### Angsana ★★★

The sister resort of Banyan Tree is funkier in its style, with lime green the prominent colour and fresh fruit used as part of the décor. Its twin attractions are its spa and its diving facilities. Guests are free to go between the two islands by boat.

*Tel: 664 0326. Email: maldives@angsana.com. www.angsana.com*

### Banyan Tree ★★★★

A top-class resort that offers high-end luxury and service with an eco-friendly touch. The shell-shaped (television-free) villas, with their private Jacuzzis and mellow music are so inspiring you may not even want to visit the beach. The on-site marine biologist is on hand to teach guests all about the delicate marine environment the hotel is working to preserve. The embargo on children under 12 makes this a peaceful haven, and quite possibly the nicest high-end resort here. Another Banyan Tree on Madivaru, in Ari Atoll, opened in the second half of 2007.

*Tel: 664 3147. Email: maldives@banyantree.com. www.banyantree.com*

### EATING OUT

### Reethi Restaurant ★★

The food miles involved must be astronomical, as the Reethi Restaurant reportedly has sushi fish from Japan, free-range lamb from Australia and strawberries from Belgium flown in fresh every week. The result is very highly rated contemporary cuisine fusing Far Eastern and Mediterranean flavours,

served in three different locations on the island, including beachside.
*Reethi Rah. Tel: 664 8800. Email: reservations@ oneandonlyresorts.com.mv. www.oneandonlyresorts. com*

**Full Moon ★★★**
The resort's selection of restaurants includes Casa Luna, a sophisticated eatery serving contemporary Mediterranean dishes including seafood and pizza, Atoll Grill, an à la carte restaurant by the beach, and Sawasdee, serving Thai and Chinese food in a romantic ambience. Its proximity to Male should allow you to visit one of its restaurants from the capital, if you call ahead to arrange it.
*Tel: 664 2010. Email: frontoffice@ fullmoon.com.mv. www.universalresorts.com*

**Kurumba ★★★**
Kurumba is one of several large resorts within an hour of Male, where, theoretically at least, it is possible to come from the capital by boat for dinner. Its

Arabian, Chinese, Indian and Mediterranean restaurants are very highly reputed, with fine food supplemented by an excellent wine list offering both European and New World wines. It could be a costly endeavour, with the meal alone likely to reach $80–100 per person, and the transport there and back not cheap either, but the quality of the cuisine should make the expense and organisational demands worthwhile.
*Tel: 664 2324. Email: kurumba@dhivehi.net.mv. www.universalresorts.com*

**Paradise Island ★★★**
Paradise's excellent Japanese restaurant has regular sushi nights and dinner is sometimes served at tables on the beach. At the end of the jetty, an equally good Italian restaurant has great views out over the ocean. The island is near enough to Male for non-guests to visit for dinner, though this would be costly and take some organisation.
*Tel: 664 0011. Email: info@paradise-*

*island.com.mv. www.villahotels.com*

**Soneva Gili ★★★★**
The no shoes ethos at Soneva Gili's top-class restaurant allows you the pleasure of combining sophisticated dining with a relaxed atmosphere. Many of the ingredients come from the island's garden – something that will please anyone with food mile concerns – and there's also an over-water restaurant. The island's fresh dishes get top marks. Meals can also be taken privately in your villa or on a sandbank.
*Tel: 664 0304. Email: sales-maldives@ sonevaresorts.com. www.sonevaresorts.com*

## Sport and leisure
### Diving
**Delphis Diving**
Friendly diving centre with capable staff whose easy manner is reassuring to beginners. There are courses and dives for novices right up to instructor level. They also rent snorkelling equipment. The firm has over 20 years of experience working in

the Maldives. It has another branch at Royal Island.
*Paradise Island.*
*Tel: 664 5243. Email: ddcpar@delphis.com.mv. www.delphisdiving.com*

**Spa**
**Huvafenfushi**
The world's first underwater spa is an astonishing architectural feat. There are two underwater rooms, and six above the sea with glass floors. A resident naturopath analyses your blood, and the facilities extend to an aroma-infused steam room, ice room, salt water flotation pool and high-tech rain shower, along with the more typical sauna, yoga pavilion and gym.
*Huvafenfushi Resort.*
*Tel: 664 4222. Email: info@huvafenfushi.com. www.huvafenfushi.com*

**SOUTH MALE ATOLL**
**ACCOMMODATION**
**Laguna Maldives ★★**
Rated by many as one of the most beautiful islands in the country, Laguna Maldives complements its natural

charms with tasteful and elegant accommodation. The spa is highly rated, and there are plenty of other ways to pass the time. Given what is on offer here, and the reasonable sums charged for it, the resort is understandably in high demand.
*Tel: 664 5903. Email: lbr@dhivehinet.net.mv. www.universalresorts.com*
**Olhuveli Beach Resort ★★**
The lookout tower is a highlight of this relaxing resort, which boasts excellent beaches and a large lagoon.
*Tel: 664 2788. Email: info@olhuveli.com.mv. www.olhuveli.com*
**Vadoo ★★**
One of the smallest islands, with just 31 rooms, it originally opened as Vadoo Diving Paradise and remains a diver's island, with five designated marine reserves among the many excellent locations (the resort reckons more than 40) in the vicinity, including the Vadhoo Channel. With many of the guests either Japanese

or divers, or both, this is not a place for late-night rowdiness, but an intimate, low-key place for those out to enjoy the ocean, the massage table or the beach.
*Tel: 664 3976. Email: vadoo@vadoo.com.mv. www.vadoo.net*
**Rihiveli Beach ★★★**
A tranquil and rustic resort with rooms fashioned out of the island's own wood. It's the southernmost resort in South Male Atoll and out of range of motorboats nipping tourists and supplies back and forth. Understandably given its peacefulness, most guests are couples after some relaxation, and the resort gets a lot of repeat trade. The two uninhabited islands within the lagoon are a nice bonus.
*Tel: 664 1994.*
*Email: reservations@ rihiveli-maldives.com. www. rihiveli-maldives.com*

**EATING OUT**
**Fihalhohi ★**
A fortnightly schedule of imaginative themed buffets makes it

impossible to get bored of eating at the Fihalhohi Resort, and the chefs are keen that guests try Maldivian fare rather than sticking unadventurously to their native cuisines. International gastronomy is covered, however; examples include 1001 Arabian Nights, the Middle Eastern buffet, and When in Rome, serving, unsurprisingly, Italian food. There's even a fish and chips night.

*Tel: 664 2903. Email: fiha@dhivehinet.net.mv. www.fihalhohi.net*

**Taj Exotica** ★★★★
Exquisitely presented Pan-Asian and continental cuisine, washed down with a choice of quality wine (with some bottles breaking the $1,000 mark). Of the island's two main restaurants, The Deep End, a Mediterranean restaurant that serves meat, game and seafood, is slightly more formal than 24 Degrees. Both charge justifiably high prices.

*Tel: 664 2200.
Email: exotica.maldives@ tajhotels.com.
www.tajhotels.com*

### Diving
**Dive Centre Laguna**
A very well-regarded dive centre run by VIT (CMAS), SSI and PADI qualified instructors. The encyclopaedic marine expertise of Herbert Unger, the renowned instructor with some three decades of experience in the Maldives, is a huge plus.

*Laguna Maldives.
Tel: 664 5903. Email: lbr@ dhivehinet.net.mv.
www.universalresorts.com*

**Diverland**
A safety-oriented and professional diving company. The Austrian-run firm can take divers to 25 sites within an hour's journey, including the Embudu Kandu Marine Area. The drift dive known as the Embudu Express is legendary in scuba circles. The company offers Nitrox and Rebreather and also offers group discounts. It

has other outlets on Gan and Summer Island.

*Embudu Village.
Tel: 777 1157.
www.diverland.com*

### Spas
**Barberyn Ayurveda Health Centre**
The Sri Lankan ayurveda practitioners take a holistic approach, so this outlet will satisfy anyone who buys into the whole ayurvedic philosophy, rather than just holidaymakers who fancy indulging themselves with a soothing massage. To this end, the chefs, who had their training in Sri Lanka, work in cooperation with the health centre to provide a complementary menu. Other options include yoga and meditation.

*Vadoo Island.
Tel: 664 3976. Email: vadoo@vadoo.com.mv.
www.vadoo.net*

**Shambhala Spa**
Cuisine, yoga and Asian healing traditions are part of the holistic approach taken by the award-winning Shambhala Spa, which even flies in famous yoga specialists

for week-long retreats. There's also a hydrotherapy pool, and the range of treatments includes some his and hers.

*Cocoa Island.*
*Tel: 664 1818. Email:*
*cocoaisland@*
*comoshambhala.bz.*
*www.comoshambhala.bz*

## ARI ATOLL

### ACCOMMODATION

#### Angaga ★★
Angaga tries to preserve the quiet island paradise beloved of honeymooners, with private dining on the beach, while still providing a range of participatory evening entertainment, such as *Bodu Beru* dancing and themed parties. There is also excellent diving and snorkelling. It attracts a professional clientele.
*Tel: 666 0510.*
*Email: angaga@*
*dhivehinet.net.mv.*
*www.angaga.com.mv*

#### Kuramathi ★★
The only island to host not one but three resorts, this diversity makes Kuramathi popular with independent travellers and anyone prone to island fever. Rasdhoo village island is only ten minutes away by *dhoni*.
*Tel: 666 0523/7/9.*
*Email: cottage@kuramathi.*
*com.mv, village@*
*kuramathi.com.mv, or*
*blagoon@kuramathi.*
*com.mv.*
*www.kuramathi.com*

#### Sun Island ★★
Awarded for its environmental friendliness, Sun Island is so large that bikes and golf buggies are required to ferry guests around. The resort attracts a young crowd, and there are plenty of bars and activities. The 21-room spa is excellent. Accommodation is divided into normal, deluxe, super deluxe, water bungalows and four presidential suites. While the main dining area is rather crowded and canteen-like, the restaurant for those in the more expensive accommodation is serene. Nearby is Holiday Island, Sun's quieter resort with an older clientele, and it's also recommended.

*Tel: 668 0088. Email:*
*info@sun-island.com.mv.*
*www.sunislandmaldives.*
*com*

#### Veligandu ★★
A classic 'feel the sand between your toes' kind of place, both the reception and restaurant have sand on the ground at this wonderfully laid-back resort. It is the natural assets – chiefly the beautiful beaches – that are the big draw here, attracting a European clientele, mainly couples, who come for the peace, the quiet and the scenery.
*Tel: 666 0519.*
*Email: reservations@*
*veliganduisland.com.*
*www.veligandu.com*

#### White Sands ★★
A relaxed resort, whose two levels of accommodation prices attract a mix of guests. As such, it is one of the more social resorts, with four restaurants and bars, and nightly entertainment includes a disco. In the daytime there's a wide range of land sports in which to participate – and participation is the name

of the game at this lively place. High occupancy levels all year round make it a wise idea to book early.
*Tel: 666 0513. Email: resort@ maldiveswhitesands.com. www.maldiveswhitesands. com*

### Conrad Maldives Rangali Island ★★★★

After upgrading in December 2007 from an 'ordinary' Hilton to become part of the hotel chain's 'luxury brand', the resort, which already counts Sir Paul McCartney among its returning regulars, looks set to become even posher. As well as upgrading one of its kitchens and wine cellar, the resort also bought another boat.
*Tel: 668 0629. Email: Maldives@hilton.com. www.hilton.com*

### EATING OUT
### Thudufushi ★★★

The food at this all-inclusive resort attracts rave reviews. Italian, Spanish, International, Mexican, BBQ, Asian and Maldivian are all covered, with lobster and prawn dishes available for a charge. Waiters are attentive and friendly, and you can dine under the stars or in an air-conditioned hall.
*Tel: 666 0583. Email: admin@thudufushi.com. mv. www.planhotel.ch*

### Ithaa Undersea Restaurant ★★★★

The Hilton's famous underwater restaurant, 5m (16ft) below sea level, is a unique dining experience which is worth breaking the bank for – and you will have to. The hotel has ensured that the incredible interior is not let down by the food; sample items on the menu include roasted Maldivian pumpkin soup with sour cream and Beluga caviar, and lobster with Maldivian beach grass (whatever that may be), lime, and red pepper sauce. Book ahead, dress up and take your credit card; the meal will cost significantly over $200 per person.
*Conrad Maldives Rangali Island. Tel: 668 0629. Email: Maldives@*

*hilton.com. www.hilton.com*

### SPORT AND LEISURE
### Diving
### Euro Divers

The Swiss company, which has over 30 years of experience, runs diving schools in three continents. Courses are available from beginner level to assistant instructor, starting at around $60 and going up to nearly $800. Its regional head office is in Male, but the branches themselves are based at White Sands, Kurumba, Velidhu, Rihiveli, Full Moon, Club Men Kani, Vilamendhoo and Eriyadu, as well as on the *Atoll Explorer* (*see panel, p93*).
*H Meerubahuruge, Ameer Ahmed Magu. Tel: 331 3868. Email: regional-maldives@ euro-divers.com. www.euro-divers.com*

### Ocean Pro Dive School

Early morning, two-tank and night dives and free Nitrox are provided by the friendly team at Ocean Pro. The Swiss-owned company has other branches at Coco Palm, Veligandu, Lily Beach, Helengeli and Meeru.

*Mirihi. Tel: 666 0500. Email: mirihi@ oceanpro-diveteam.com. www.oceanpro-diveteam.com*

### Sub Aqua

The German diving school chain runs Ellaidhoo's operation, with courses for divers of all (and no) abilities, including Nitrox, Draeger Atlantis 1 SCR and Buddy Inspiration CCR courses and PADI, NAUI, ANDI and RAB certificates. The excellent house reef is typical of the quality of diving available in the area, and the island has become a well-known diver's resort.

*Ellaidhoo. Tel: 666 0586. Email: info@ellaidhoo. com.mv. www.travelin-maldives.com*

## Spa
### Araamu Spa

The spa can accommodate up to 31 customers at a time, the majority of whom are couples. Drawing on local, ayurvedic and European techniques, the menu reaches 100 different treatments that detox, de-stress and beautify. Anyone willing to put in some serious spa time can do the week-long package. The same company operates smaller facilities at Paradise and Royal islands.

*Sun Island. Tel: 668 0088. www.araamuspa.com*

## NORTHERN ATOLLS
### ACCOMMODATION
### Meedhupparu ★★

The first and only resort in Raa Atoll has gloriously expansive beaches and a plethora of on-site facilities – ayurveda centre, spa, sauna, Jacuzzi, hairdressing salon plus jewellery and clothes shopping – that will please anyone who wants to combine island relaxation with mainland convenience and choice. Plenty of participatory evening activities are laid on, and the largely Italian customer base ensures a cheerful, lively atmosphere.

*Tel: 658 7700. Email: re@ meedhupparu.com.mv. www.aitkenspenceholidays. com*

### Royal Island ★★★

This northern getaway fully deserves its regal appellation. The atmosphere is peaceful and sophisticated, the superb buffet includes treats such as sushi and the wooden rooms have been embellished with substantial, high-quality furnishings that you would not normally expect at a beach resort. The professional management also take their environmental responsibilities very seriously. Little wonder that the two splendid presidential suites are popular with the great and the good.

*Tel: 660 0088. Email: info@royal-island.com. www.royal-island.com*

### EATING OUT
### Kuredu ★

Steak and seafood, Thai and Italian restaurants are set off by Tea House, a Maldivian café serving local snacks and curries. True to tradition, no alcohol is served. No need to panic – there are six separate bars on the island.

*Tel: 662 0337. Email: reservations@kuredu.com. www.kuredu.com*

**Reethi Beach ★★**

The four highly rated restaurants at Reethi Beach make good use of the island's herb, fruit and vegetable garden. Rehendhi Restaurant blends Eastern and Western flavours and includes a healthfood corner. Reethi Grill will delight carnivores with its barbecues, and also holds Mongolian nights. Dhivehi Restaurant pitches itself as the first restaurant in the country to offer exclusively Maldivian cuisine. And Huvandhumaa is a traditional Chinese restaurant, complete with painted dragons.

*Tel: 660 2626. Email: info@reethibeach.com.mv. www.reethibeach.com*

**Kanuhura ★★★**

With a reputation for serving some of the best food throughout the archipelago, Kanuhura's chefs cook at open stations preparing themed food and responding to individual requests. Fish, obviously, is a key theme, as are local dishes, and foodies can also choose from sushi, fusion cuisine and produce from all over the world. Kanuhura also makes its own ice cream. It is sometimes possible to eat on the beach, overlooking the lagoon.

*Tel: 664 8800. Email: reservations@ oneandonlyresorts.com.mv. www.oneandonlyresorts. com*

**Royal Island ★★★**

The sophisticated restaurant at Royal Island makes sure to seat its guests at a discrete distance apart. The muted yet classy design gives it a far more grown-up feel than the typical beachside eatery, and the professionalism and friendliness of the staff are exemplary. The buffet is a higher-quality version of the standard Maldivian resort fare, with unexpected delights such as sushi.

*Tel: 660 0088. Email: info@royal-island.com. www.royal-island.com*

SPORT AND LEISURE

### Diving

**Pro Divers**

Pro Divers seems to be embracing the expansionist ethos of Western adventure sports companies and has released its own range of clothing. Other services include a video lab and Nitrox. The company has outlets on Kuredu, Komandoo and Vakarufalhi (Ari Atoll).

*Champa Building, Kandidhonmaniku Goalhi, Male. Tel: 662 0343. Email: info@prodivers.com. www.prodivers.com*

### Spa

**Six Senses Spa**

The people at Six Senses are so confident of the quality of their services that guests get half an hour's worth of free treatment. Health and beauty treatments, some of which can be administered in your villa, use both Western and Eastern methods, including ayurveda. Another outlet is open on Soneva Gili, in North Male Atoll.

Soneva Fushi.
Tel: 660 0304. Email:
mgr-fushi@sixsensespas.
com. www.sixsenses.com

## SOUTHERN ATOLLS

### ACCOMMODATION

**Equator Village ★**

Equator Village is a
beacon for independent
(and low-budget)
travellers in the package-
holiday-dominated
Maldives. With a long
bridge that connects Gan,
where the resort is based
in a converted British
army mess, to three other
village islands, including
the atoll capital, there is
plenty of antidote to
island fever and an
opportunity to see
Maldivian life as it is.
Tel: 689 8721.
Email: equator@
dhivehinet.net.mv.
www.equatorvillage.com

**Angsana Velavaru
Island ★★**

A marvellous new palm-
covered resort with
beautiful beaches. The
buildings have been
designed to blend in
harmoniously with the
island's natural charms.
Tel: 676 0028. Email:
reservations-maldives@

velavaru.com.
www.velavaru.com

**Herathera ★★**

Recently opened in Seenu
Atoll, this unusually long
and thin island offers
4km (2¹/₂ miles) of beach
and enough foliage for a
nature trail and garden
tours, with three
swimming pools and a
variety of land sports,
including tennis and
football. A spa, diving
centre and water sports
will feature. The nightly
entertainment and large
number of rooms (300),
along with three
different bars are likely
to make this one of the
more happening resorts.
Tel: 689 7766.
Email: reservations@
herathera.com.
www.herathera.com

### EATING OUT

**Filitheyo ★★★**

The resort's award-
winning buffet includes
a generous selection of
Maldivian and
international dishes.
The desserts are
particularly good. À la
carte dishes are available
in the Sunset Restaurant
next to the pool.

Tel: 331 6131.
Email: fili@aaa.com.mv.
www.aaa-resortsmaldives.
com

### SPORT AND LEISURE

**Diving**

**GI Diving**

As the resort name
suggests, Alimatha
Aquatic gives paramount
importance to diving and
water-sports enthusiasts.
The island's diving
centre caters for both
beginners and pros. The
windsurfing and sailing
are also good here.
Alimatha Aquatic Resort.
Email: info@tgidiving.com
www.tgidiving.com

**Werner Lau**

A professional and
friendly centre that offers
Barakuda (CMAS), SSI
and PADI courses. There
are night dives,
underwater cameras, and
the incipient state of
tourism here means that,
for now, divers can enjoy
the 30 sites without an
underwater crowd. Other
sites are at Eriyadu and
Filitheyo.
Medhufushi. Tel: 672 0026.
Email: medhufushi@
wernerlau.com.
www.wernerlau.com

# Index

**A**

accommodation 116–17, 132 see also individual locations
air travel 21, 72, 82–3, 114, 134
alcohol 10, 121, 134
Alimatha Aquatic Resort 96, 98, 157
Andre, Andreas 40
Angaga 72, 74, 153
Angsana Ihuru (North Male Atoll) 44–6, 149
Angsana Velavaru (Southern Atolls) 98–9, 157
architecture 14–15, 22, 28, 29, 32–3, 41, 61, 78
Ari Atoll 72–81, 107, 153–5
Artificial Beach 32
Asdu Sun Island 148
Atoll Explorer 93, 123–4
atoll formation 6, 42–3
atoll names 108

**B**

banana boating 130–1
Banana Reef 48
Bandos 46–7, 148
Banyan Tree 45, 47–8, 71, 149
Baros 48
beaches
    Ari Atoll 78
    Male 32
    North Male Atoll 54
    Northern Atolls 89
    South Male Atoll 62
birds 66, 103, 149
black magic 56–7
boats 24, 54, 64, 68–9, 72, 75, 93, 94, 100, 107, 112–13, 114, 117, 123–4, 128
Bodu Beru (music) 17, 122
Bolifushi 58
Borgo, Giovanni 78
British Council 146–7
British Loyalty, The 100
British War Memorial Garden 102
business facilities 50, 51, 149

**C**

cafés 124, 145, 146
cemetery 102
Chaaya Lagoon Hakura Huraa 99
Chandanee Magu 32
children 54, 95, 102, 132–3
cinema 15, 147
climate 28, 94, 110–11
Club Rannalhi 58–9

Coco Palm Resort (Northern Atolls) 86, 88, 107
Cocoa Island Resort (South Male Atoll) 59–61, 152–3
coconut 120
Conrad Maldives Rangali Island 74–5, 154
consulates 143
coral items 126
coral structures 42, 43, 71, 84–5, 95
    North Male Atoll 44, 48, 50, 52
    South Male Atoll 61
    Southern Atolls 99–100, 101
cowries 30–1
crab racing 124
crafts 15–16, 126
credit cards 127
crime 142
cruises 24, 68–9, 93, 117
culture 14–17, 22, 28, 29, 32–3, 38–9, 41, 48–9, 61, 78, 96, 122–4, 126, 146–7 see also folklore; local life
culture shock 26
currency 30–1, 135
customs 126–7, 134
cycling 102–3, 114

**D**

dance 17, 122–4
Darwin, Charles 42–3
Dhigali Haa 93
Dhiggiri 100
Dhoni Mighili 75, 107
dhonis (boats) 68–9, 75, 107, 113
Didi, Mohamed Amin 49
disabilities 139
discrete tourism 5, 64, 65, 68, 112 see also local life
diving 23–4, 69, 94–5, 104, 111, 128
    Ari Atoll 72, 79, 80–1, 154–5
    Male 147
    North Male Atoll 48, 49, 50, 150–1
    Northern Atolls 86, 88–9, 90, 93, 156
    South Male Atoll 61, 62–3, 152
    Southern Atolls 96, 98, 100, 101, 157
dolphin watching 128
dress 36
drink 10, 121, 134
driving 114
duty 126–7

**E**

eating out 122, 132–3
    Ari Atoll 74, 154
    Male 145–6
    North Male Atoll 149–50
    Northern Atolls 155–6
    South Male Atoll 151–2
    Southern Atolls 99, 157
eels 34
Eid 18
Eidhigali Kilhi 103
electricity 134
Ellaidhoo 155
embassies 143
Embudu 61, 152
emergencies 142–3
entertainment 15, 122–5
    Ari Atoll 81
    Male 146–7
    North Male Atoll 22, 44, 50–1, 148–9
    Northern Atolls 89
    South Male Atoll 58
entry formalities 134, 136
environmentalism 6, 45–6, 47, 67, 70–1, 84, 85, 93
Equator Village 100–1, 157
Esjehi Art Gallery 146
etiquette 36, 120
events 18–19

**F**

fauna and flora 50, 66–7, 103, 149 see also marine life
ferries 54, 114
Fesdu 107
festivals 18–19
Fihalhohi Tourist Resort 61, 151–2
Filitheyo 100, 157
fish 21, 34, 49, 67, 72, 104–5, 118–19, 120
fish feeding 128–9
fishing 86
flora and fauna 50, 66–7, 103, 149 see also marine life
folklore 11, 16, 24, 27, 56–7, 120
food and drink 10, 18–19, 21, 34–5, 44, 118–21, 134, 142 see also eating out
football 55, 129, 147
Full Moon 48, 150

**G**

gambling 124
Gan 96, 100–1, 102
gardens 40–1, 102
Gayoom, Maumoon Abdul 13, 52
gender issues 15, 124

geography 6, 43
Giravaru 48–50, 148
guest houses 144
Guraidhoo 124

**H**

Halaveli 75–6
health 133, 136, 142
hedhikaa (snacks) 120
Herathera 157
history 8–9, 27, 30–1, 40, 42–3, 78, 90, 100, 137
Hithadhoo 103
Holiday Island 75–6
hospitals 142
Hukuru Miskiiy 29, 36–7
Huvafenfushi Resort 151

**I**

Ibn Battuta 90
Idu Miskiiy 37
industry 44
insurance 142
Inter Atoll Travel Permit 64
internet 16–17, 134–5
Islam 10–11, 18–19, 28, 29, 33, 36–7, 56, 134, 137
Islamic Centre 28, 32–3
Island Hideaway 88–9
island hopping 23–4, 64–5, 112
island rentals 107–8

**J**

jetskiing 130–1
Jumhooree Binaa 28
Jumhooree Maidhaan 28

**K**

Kanuhura 156
kneeboarding 130–1
Koattey 103
Komandoo 89
Kuda Haa 49
Kuramathi 76–7, 153
Kuramba 50, 149, 150
Kuredu Resort 89–90, 155–6
Kurumba 50, 149, 150

**L**

lacquerware 15–16, 126
Laguna Maldives 61–2, 151, 152
language 17, 140–1
Lily Beach 78
Lion's Head 49
literature 16–17
lizards 66–7
local life 5, 16, 22, 26, 32, 34, 35, 54, 64–5, 102, 108, 118–20, 124–5

**M**

Maamigili 76
Male 24, 26–9, 32–41, 114, 117, 124–5, 144–8

mapping 43
maps 7, 20
    Ari Atoll 73
    cruise routes 69
    Male 27, 29
    North Male Atoll 45, 55
    Northern Atolls 87
    seaplane routes 83
    South Male Atoll 59
    Southern Atolls 97, 103
marine life 21, 49, 61, 63, 67, 71, 72, 104–5, 128–9
    see also coral structures; fish
markets 34–5
mats 15, 126
Medhufushi 101
media 13, 125, 138
Medu Miskiiy 37
Meedhupparu 90, 155
Meeru 50–1
money 127, 135
monsoons 94, 110, 111
mosques 15
    Male 28, 29, 32–3, 36–7, 41
    North Male Atoll 54, 55
    Southern Atolls 102
motorbikes 114
Mulee-Aage 29
museums 38–9, 146
music 17, 122–4

N
names for atolls 108
National Library 146–7
National Museum 38–9
nightlife 22, 44, 50–1, 58, 81, 122–4, 147
Nika Island Resort 78–9
North Male Atoll 22, 23–4, 44–55, 71, 107–8, 148–51
Northern Atolls 71, 82, 86–93, 107, 155–7

O
ocean sunfish 105
Old Mosque (Villigilli) 54

Olhuveli Beach Resort 151
opening hours 10, 127, 136

P
package holidays 134
Paradise Island 51, 148–9, 150–1
parasailing 130–1
parks and gardens 28, 40–1, 102
passports 136
People's Majlis 29
pharmacies 136, 142
politics 9, 12–13, 52
population 26
post 136–7
public holidays 18–19, 137
Pyrard de Laval, François 137

R
Ramadan 18
reading 137–8
recycling 71
Redhin 61
Reethi Beach 91–2, 156
Reethi Rah 107, 149–50
religion 8, 38, 96 see also Islam
renting islands 107–8
reserves and sanctuaries 49, 93, 103
restaurants 74, 122, 132–3, 154 see also eating out
Rihiveli Beach 62, 151
Royal Island Resort 92–3, 155, 156

S
safari boats 24, 68–9, 107, 117
safety 116, 131, 132, 133, 142
sanctuaries and reserves 49, 93, 103
seaplanes 21, 72, 82–3, 114
seasons 110–11
sharks 67, 72, 105
ships see boats
shopping 32, 34–5, 65, 99, 126–7

smoking 124, 137
snacks 120
snorkelling 104, 130
Soneva Fushi Resort (Northern Atolls) 93, 156–7
Soneva Gili Resort (North Male Atoll) 51–2, 107–8, 150
South Male Atoll 21, 23–4, 58–63, 151–3
Southern Atolls 82, 96–103, 108, 124, 157
spas and treatments 130
    Ari Atoll 74, 80, 155
    Male 147–8
    North Male Atoll 22, 151
    Northern Atolls 88, 156–7
    South Male Atoll 152–3
speedboats 64, 107, 113
sport and activities 23–4, 69, 94–5, 104, 111, 128–31, 133, 142
    Ari Atoll 72, 74, 75, 76, 78–9, 80–1, 154–5
    Male 147–8
    North Male Atoll 22, 44–5, 47, 48, 49, 50, 51, 52, 55, 150–1
    Northern Atolls 86, 88–9, 90, 91–2, 93, 156–7
    South Male Atoll 21, 58, 61, 62–3, 152–3
    Southern Atolls 96, 98, 100, 101, 157
submarine ride 148
Sultan Park 28, 40–1
Sultan's Palace 40
Sun Island Resort 79–80, 153, 155
surfing 130
swimming 133, 142

T
Taj Exotica 62–3, 152
tax 138
taxis 114

teahouses 124
telephones 138–9
Theemuge 41
Thudufushi 80, 154
Thulhaagiri 52–3, 149
time 139
tipping 121
toilets 139
tours 23–4, 64–5, 68–9, 93, 94, 112
trade 30–1
tuna 120
turtles 67, 71
TV 125

U
underwater restaurant 74, 154
underwater spa 74, 151
uninhabited islands 64, 107–8

V
Vadhoo Channel 58, 62, 63
Vadoo 63, 151, 152
Velidhu 80–1
Veligandu 153
Vilamendhoo Island Resort 81
village islands 108
Villingili 54–5
Villingili Mosque 55
Vilu Reef Resort 101
visas 136

W
wakeboarding 130–1
walks 112
    Male 28–9
    North Male Atoll 54–5
    Southern Atolls 102–3
water bungalows 116–17
waterskiing 130–1
whale watching 128
White Sands 81, 153–4

Y
yachts 107

# Acknowledgements

Thomas Cook Publishing wishes to thank Vasile Szakacs for the photographs in this book, to whom the copyright belongs, except for the following images:

CHAAYA LAGOON HAKURA HURAA 99
DREAMSTIME.COM/Matthias Nordmeyer 63
FILITHEYO ISLAND RESORT 101
FLICKR/Simiant 49, eNil 67, 89
BRIAN MCMORROW 32, 36, 38, 39, 50
PICTURES COLOUR LIBRARY 60
WIKIMEDIA COMMONS/Fizan 18, Bricktop 31
WORLD PICTURES/PHOTOSHOT 1, 13, 75

For CAMBRIDGE PUBLISHING MANAGEMENT LTD:
**Project editor**: Rosalind Munro
**Typesetter**: Paul Queripel
**Proofreader**: Dick Lloyd-Williams
**Indexer**: Karolin Thomas

## SEND YOUR THOUGHTS TO
## BOOKS@THOMASCOOK.COM

We're committed to providing the very best up-to-date information in our travel guides and constantly strive to make them as useful as they can be. You can help us to improve future editions by letting us have your feedback. If you've made a wonderful discovery on your travels that we don't already feature, if you'd like to inform us about recent changes to anything that we do include, or if you simply want to let us know your thoughts about this guidebook and how we can make it even better – we'd love to hear from you.

Send us ideas, discoveries and recommendations today and then look out for your valuable input in the next edition of this title.

Emails to the above address, or letters to Travellers Series Editor, Thomas Cook Publishing, PO Box 227, Coningsby Road, Peterborough PE3 8SB, UK.

Please don't forget to let us know which title your feedback refers to!